Emotionally Immature Parents

A Practical Guide to Recognize and Overcome Childhood Emotional Neglect and Lack of Empathy from Absent and Self-Involved Parents

Rose Mary Parker

Copyright © 2020 All rights reserved

Emotionally Immature Parents

Emotionally Immature Parents

All rights reserved, including the right to reproduce this book or portions thereof in any form whatsoever

Under no circumstances will any blame or legal responsibility be held against the publisher, or author, for any damages, reparation, or monetary loss due to the information contained with this book, either directly or indirectly.

Legal Notice:

This book is copyright protected. It is only for personal use. You cannot use, sell, distribute, amend, paraphrase, or quote any content of the book, without the consent of the publisher or author.

Disclaimer Notice:

The information contained herein this book is for entertainment and educational purposes only. All effort has been executed to present up to date, reliable, complete, and accurate information. The content with this book comes from several sources. Please consult a licensed professional before using any technique outlined in this document.

The reader agrees that the author is not responsible, directly or indirectly, for issues, that are incurred as a result of the use of the information contained with this document, including, but not limited to errors, omissions, or inaccuracies.

All rights reserved, including the right to reproduce this book or portions thereof in any form whatsoever.

Copyright © 2020 Rose Mary Parker

Emotionally Immature Parents

Emotionally Immature Parents

TABLE OF CONTENT

INTRODUCTION 1

Chapter 1: Importance of Parenting 7

1.1 How to Become a Good Parent to Your Children 14

Chapter 2: Personality Traits of Emotionally Immature Parents............................29

Chapter 3: Deep wounds left by Emotionally Immature parents...........................63

Chapter 4: How Emotional wound passed on through Family Ties 75

Chapter 5: Analyzing (or screening) types of Emotionally Immature Parents.....81

Chapter 6: Children born Adult: Different Children reactions 101

Chapter 7: Recognizing the problem awaking from the nightmare.....................111

Chapter 8: Being an Internalizer 125

Chapter 9: Dealing with Emotionally Immature Parents Aging...........................149

Chapter 10: Reclaiming your freedom to be Yourself 167

10.1 Living Your Own Life Free From An Emotionally Immature Parent 182

Chapter 11: Healing (Specialist and Self-Help) 197

Chapter 12: How to recognize an Emotionally Mature Relationship 217

CONCLUSION 237

INTRODUCTION

I am sure that out of the first five most memorable childhood memories, at least two will be about your parents. The evening walks, the weekend trips, the surprise gifts, and the unconditional love and support - parents have so much to give to us. And by 'parents', I do not mean only the biological father and mother. Parental love can come from biological parents, surrogate or foster parents, or parental figures like grandparents, uncles, and aunts, or other close relatives.

Parents shape our lives - but not in the way we always think. It is not just the love and support from parents that helps in making us what we are, it is a lot more than that. Parents, especially the mother, is our first contact in the real world. Everything from their touch to their tone and the time they spend with us forms the basis of how we learn to interpret the world around us. And this is a big reason why different children who are raised with different parenting styles show stark variations in their temperamental qualities.

When it comes to maturity, the norm is that adults are emotionally mature ones and children are childish. But what if I told you that the roles can be reversed? There are children who are more emotionally mature than their parents and end up playing the roles parents should!

These types of parents are emotionally immature parents, and they are more prominent than you may think. A child born into a family with these kinds of parents will lead to emotional abandonment in these kids.

As children, the need for an emotional connection is stronger, and it is also essential for a child to develop healthily. In essence, once this is absent, it can lead to an emotional void that will affect the kids in more ways than one. If you are in this situation, then understand that you are not alone.

Emotionally immature parents are unable to make real connections with their kids. They also prevent these kids from expressing the emotions they feel and may blame, criticize, and make them feel less than they are. What's more, they do not care about the emotional state of their children, all of which have a ripple effect on the kids.

For anyone who has dealt with all of these, it will be vital for you to address all of the negative impacts left behind by these parents. And your healing should be a priority. In this book, we will be looking into who emotionally immature parents are, and all you need to know about them.

Thank you for choosing Emotionally Immature Parents. I hope you will find useful information about your awareness and life changing. I would appreciate hearing your thoughts with a short review on Amazon.

Emotionally Immature Parents

Emotionally Immature Parents

Chapter 1: Importance of Parenting

Parenting already is a tough job for a person, couple that with having to communicate with a teenager or adolescent that doesn't want to communicate with you. Then, you know you have an arduous job on your hands. One aspect of parenting where a lot of parents have failed in is communicating with their kids, and who can blame them; they are just mirroring the way they were spoken to as a child. Parents don't have any problem giving instructions and facts to their kids; trust me! They excel at that. Things like "Go and clean my car." Or: "Make sure you look out for cars before crossing the road." Of course, parents excel at this form of communication. Do you want to know where parents fail? When it comes to the emotional stuff, parents really suck at communicating their intense feelings – or when their child's feelings are involved? Many parents say they don't just struggle with communicating with their child; they complain that even when they initiate a conversation, their kids only reply with one-word answers or nods, or the monosyllabic yes/no answers. The real struggle is actually having a true dialogue with your kids when they feel like they can actually tell you what it is that bothers them, and you as their parents can advise them on what to do and, in some cases, just listen.

Here are some Tips on Parenting:

Choose discipline over punishment

When your child displays a behavioral pattern that is abhorrent and/or unusual, before you impulsively send them to the dungeon; You should at least try to understand why they did what they did and then let them know why the way they are reacting to it is bad. This is possibly one of the best chances you would get to nip bad behavior in the bud, so why waste it? This way, you communicate to your child that they can approach you when things don't seem to be going how they expect, and also when they are excited about something, they will be inclined to let you know, too.

Acknowledge their emotions

Sometimes we know that our kids are just little brats about their emotions and we can sometimes make the mistake of just dismissing those emotions, by saying things like, "Oh, stop being such a brat" or "You are just saying that because you are still a kid." These are how we push them away gradually. Even if the way they are acting is just a result of childish emotions, we should find a way to acknowledge that we know how they feel and that it gets better with time. That way, when they face the real adversities that come during the teenage years, then they will know that they can always speak with their parents.

You should note, however, that all of these are general ways to deal with fostering excellent communication with your child. It varies from child to child, as they have different personalities, upbringing, environment, and so many more factors. When it comes down to it, though, this is the basic principle behind being in a proper communicative relationship with your kid.

Now that you know how to make sure you don't prevent your kids from being able to communicate with you, you might wonder just how to communicate with your kids. Some of the ways that works are as follows;

Using approaching statements

Generally, these are the statements that allow your children to want to say more. This could work on almost anybody, but focus! We are talking about our children here! The whole idea is to let your child know that you are really interested in what he/she has to say. These kinds of statements allow your children to see that you accept and respect him/her; it makes it feel more natural to talk to you. Some of the kinds of "approaching statements" you can use include:

- Oh, I see,
- How about that!
- Wow! Really?
- I really would like to know more,
- What! No way.
- Amazing.
- Woah!
- That's cool.
- Are you serious, so what happened next?

Now, I am not saying you have to fake this sort of response when you are with your kid, because trust me, they can easily sense when you are not sincere with them. What you need to do is practice actually listening to them when they speak and when they expect to get a response from you; if you have been listening, you will be able to respond in a way similar to the ones listed above. Also, you should know that in making them feel that you care, eye contact is actually necessary. If you make an exclamation and you are not looking up from the cabbage that you are slicing, it would not matter that you listened. The keyword here is attention.

Tell your kids what to "do" a lot more than "what not to do"

A lot of parents actually make the mistake of always telling their kids what not to do, while this is necessary and okay sometimes. One thing we as parents forget is the fact that if we keep telling them what not to do, how then do they know what to do? Bear in mind the fact that it is not every time that doing the opposite of what you are told not to do becomes the right thing to do. Plus, if as a child you hear a lot of what you should not do, you tend to do those things most of the time. Also, it would help the self-esteem of your kid, if you refrain from always telling them what not to do. Instead, you should tell them what you expect them to do more often. Imagine how you would tell your friend or a relative of what not to do. You probably would instead suggest what they should do. You would say things like:

· "Hey, come on. Why not put your clothes on the dresser, they will stay less wrinkled that way?"

· "Drive carefully, Bob!"

· So, when talking to your kids, your statements should sound more like,

· "Hey, go clean your room."

· "Pick your clothes off the floor or hang them on the dresser instead."

· "Come on, John. Play your games after you are done with your assignments."

- There are some things that are reserved primarily as a warning and you should tell them straight away not to do, like:
- "Don't play with fire. It would burn you."

Bad parenting can affect a child in the following ways;

- Lack of empathy to others
- Psychological disorders
- Development of criminal behavior
- It can lead to depression and anxiety.
- Hard creating lasting relationship and friendship.
- Development of autism

1.1 How to Become a Good Parent to Your Children

Since your parents failed to raise you in the right manner, you probably want to ensure that your child does not go through the same as you. The early stages of your child's life have a lot of influence on the remainder of their life. From the instant they are born, they begin to take in the world around them. They look up to you for guidance, and this means you have a very vital role to play in ensuring the early parts of their lives go the way they should. You have the role of ensuring they develop emotionally, physically, and socially. Emotional development involves the way we express and control emotions. It also has to do with the way a person feels about themselves and others around them. Social development has to do with how we interact with others around us. While physical development has to do with how we take care of our physical bodies, proper development of all of these can ensure there is a balance in the life of a kid. If a child can develop good and healthy relationships with family and parents, they will be able to understand how to listen and coexist appropriately with others. They will also have the right level of self-confidence that will be needed to navigate the world they are in. Like we have mentioned earlier, all of these can have an impact on the overall life of the child. For this reason, you must be willing to do everything possible to ensure they develop all of these in a healthy manner, which is something your emotionally immature parent was unable to do for you.

Do Not Compare Your Kids

No matter how subtle you make it, comparing your child with other children is not the way to go. All children develop differently, and some may begin walking earlier than others. Your friend's kid may start walking earlier than yours, but this does not mean something is wrong with your kid. It's not healthy to use another kid as a milestone for yours. From thinking about it, you may unknowingly start to voice it out and act it. This will tell how you treat your kid in the long run.

Comparison has never helped anyone to be a better parent. Even as an adult, there are people in the same age bracket as you who are much better at some activities than you. Does this make them better? Or make you less important? The same analogy should be used when dealing with your children too.

If you have more than one kid, comparisons can result in your tagging your kids. For example, if you have a kid who loves sports more, you may tag him as "Our Athlete." Or one who loves reading as "Our Little Professor." Giving you kids labels like these may not necessarily be a bad thing, but if you start to equate a kid to a specific label, the other sibling may never try to meet up. This is because they may feel there is no point in trying since their sibling has already taken up that role.

Acknowledge Their Feelings

Emotionally immature parents have no empathy. They can't understand the way their kids feel, and this makes it impossible to validate these feelings. Even if their kids open up about pain or anger, these parents don't listen with empathy. Instead, they may put them down, and the kids grow up to believe it is not proper to have these sorts of emotions. This can harm the child later in the future.

Let Your Child Choose How to Play

As a parent, suggesting an activity for your kid to do regularly can be tempting. This could be in the form of recommended games and directing how a game should go. Sometimes, it is fine to do nothing and let your kid take the lead. Let them decide how to play and the way they want to play. They should do everything without any interference from you.

This is an excellent method for kids to play because they can tap into their creative spirits to determine how to have fun. This can also ensure the healthy development of the brain, which is vital for any kid to grow properly. In addition to this, it helps in developing the problem-solving skills and leadership skills of your kids since they will have full charge of their activity.

Even if you are tempted to partake, hold on till your child requests that you play with him. Doing this will make them understand a little about boundaries, and that their opinions matter. But try not to get carried away when you join in, remember that your child should be in control, as it is his activity after all.

Be a Role Model

Children pick up a lot of things from the adults around them. Even if you are not aware, they are always observing you and learning from you. This means the way you act around your children will have a significant influence on them.

From the way you respond to stressful situations, to the way you deal with anger, to how you interact with other people around you, your child is always watching. This way, they will see how you react to various circumstances and adopt it in their lives too.

Don't just be the one who says one thing and does something else. Behave in the manner you want your kids to behave. Be sure that you are responding to situations and others healthily, and your kid will do the same too.

Let Your Child Learn from Mistakes

You notice your child playing with his remote-controlled toy car, and you observe that with the direction he is headed, his toy car is going to tilt over. You hurry up to stop him from making this mistake and explain to him why it pays to slow down when going through a curved path.

Your intentions at this point may be good, but sometimes you need to allow your child to learn from their mistakes. Sometimes the experience is the best teacher anyone can have. Making these types of mistakes growing up can allow your child to properly understand that there are consequences to the actions they take. Instead of protecting them from these mistakes, let them feel the effects and learn from it.

Give Them Compliments When Due

Similar to how your actions influence your kids, the things you say to them also do the same. What you say to your kids can have a significant influence on their self-esteem. Give them compliments when they deserve it. Regardless of how insignificant the feat they have achieved may seem, giving them these compliments will make them feel pride and can boost their self-esteem. This is different from the way constant shaming and snide comments from emotionally immature parents can make a kid feel inadequate and irrelevant. Some statements can cause damage to your kids in the long run. Comments like "Why don't you make smart choices?" or "Why do you always act like a baby?" can be more damaging to your kids because they attack the self-esteem.

Spend Time with Your Kids

Working a busy job and running a family is no easy feat. For many parents, time is a luxury they can't afford to give anyone, and their kids are no exception. However, for a kid to be well-rounded and balanced, he or she has to spend some time around their parents. Attention is something a lot of kids cherish even if they don't voice it out. If you fail to give your kids the right level of attention, they may try to get it by being truants or through other harmful behaviors. Even if you can only spare 20 minutes daily, try to find some time to spend with your kids. This can help you both connect in a much more profound manner. Attention is very crucial, especially when a child is younger. However, when they get older, they may not need as much attention because they are also caught up with their own lives. These could include school classes, sports, after-school classes, and so on.

Encourage Proper Communication

Communication is essential for any healthy relationship. This makes it a necessary concept to teach your kids. You want to ensure you communicate with your kids as a parent if you want them to do something. Taking the time to properly let them understand your reason for wanting them to do something gives them an opportunity to develop and learn. Don't just enforce your instructions on them, instead explain the reasons behind your choices. If you have a problem with them, don't dish out punishments without explanations. Instead, explain to them and let them know how you feel. You could also ask their opinions regarding the best course of action. If your child makes a suggestion, don't wave it off as unimportant. Instead, consider it and see how you both can reach a favorable agreement. Children who take part in decisions will be more inclined to see them through to the end.

Adapt and Be Willing to Change

If you observe that your child is not meeting up to your expectations regarding his or her behavior, then you may want to look into these expectations. They may be unrealistic, and you may have to make some changes to them.

Sometimes the way children behave is an influence of their environment. So, a great way to change the behavior of your kid may be to make a few changes to their environment. If you observe that you are continually scolding your kid for breaking some particular set of rules, a good option may be to alter these rules a bit. There is a considerable chance that you could come up with something beneficial for you both and reduce your disagreements.

Furthermore, as your child grows older, you may slowly need to alter your style of parenting. There is a huge possibility that the things that are providing results for your kids presently may not work later on. Your kids may not look up to you as much for the guidance, but this does not mean you should stop trying to make a connection with them.

Know Your Requirements as a Parent

You certainly have areas you excel and those you don't. You will have to recognize your capacities and create achievable expectations for yourself and your kids. You don't need to have solutions to everything, so forgive yourself when you make errors. Also, remember that parenting is a broad role that requires a lot of effort from you. Don't try to deal with every area at the same time, but instead, pay attention to those that are most critical. Be truthful to yourself when you are stressed and do things you desire that will make you happy. Take a break and instead do something for you. This does not make you a bad or selfish parent. Instead, it makes you someone who knows that their well-being is crucial. This is another way to teach your kids a valuable lesson.

Even if you are always preoccupied, don't forget that your kids still remember the smallest and seemingly insignificant efforts.

Emotionally Immature Parents

Notes:

Emotionally Immature Parents

Emotionally Immature Parents

Chapter 2: Personality Traits of Emotionally Immature Parents

They are selfish: Becoming an adult is realizing that the world belongs to you as well as other people and that others need to have their own needs met too. But immature people never got this memo. They believe the world revolves around them only; their wants, their needs, their desires, their comfort, their plans, their job, etc. It's all ME, ME, ME!

To an immature person, he does not believe that anything should be out of his reach. This makes them hurt others as they never care about anyone that gets hurt in the process of achieving their aim as long as they get what they want. Having a relationship with an immature person means that you will always have your own plans and desires on the back burner while they expect you to attend to theirs.

They are commitment-phobic: Being committed to someone or something is being dedicated to that person or thing. It means you will put in efforts to make that thing a success even if it costs you. It is a sign of the strength of character and found among mature people.

For emotionally immature people, on the other hand, they never commit whether to a person, a cause, an idea, a relationship, or even a job. They cannot deprive themselves or sacrifice to get to a goal as they lack the restraint to deny themselves of anything.

They blame others: We all make mistakes at one point or another, but an adult will be ready to accept the blame for any wrongdoing, error, or oversight. Not so an immature person. Like children, afraid of repercussions or punishment and pointing the finger at others, immature people shift blame to the people around them. They are so interested in maintaining a pristine image and will rather blame an innocent person than admit a fault. Do not be surprised if you have an immature person as a colleague, and they always blamed a failed project on you.

They are not fully independent: Immature people see others as a means of achieving whatever they may desire. They do not love or care about others but will have other people in their lives because they need something from those people.

By making others feel they (immature people) depend on them (mature people), they establish a pattern of dependency that guilt the mature individual into always giving in to the whims and desires of the immature person. They will use this leverage without compunction or feeling shame. Others are depended on to take the blame for their failures, to take up their responsibilities in a team project, etc.

They are financially irresponsible: When you give a small child some money, the first thing she considers is buying candy or a pretty hair accessory. Saving and money management is not a thing little child ever give a thought to. This is the same with immature adults. They are always impulsive and do not believe in delaying gratification for any reason. They will, therefore, go ahead to buy an expensive gadget without giving any thought to how it will affect their budget for the month or go for an unplanned vacation purely on a whim. As long as their immediate desire gets satisfied, they do not care about the cost.

This also makes them terrible investors as they lack the objectivity to analyze financial investments and weigh consequences accurately. If an investment does not yield quick financial gain, an immature person will not consider it.

They are not flexible

Emotionally immature individuals are rigid. They do not like to change their minds, especially when it involves making decisions that have to do with their emotions. The same applies to their relationships as well. Instead of dealing with a problem head-on, they try to alter the situation into something more manageable for them.

To them, there is only a single solution to a problem. The instant they have made up their minds, they are not open to change. This becomes worse when another individual has an opinion that is different from theirs as they can become very irritated and defensive.

Only what they feel is best goes

As we grow older, we learn that what we want to do is not always the best option. This is why typical adults are open to considering ideas from others before they make a move. But in the emotionally immature individual, this is different since they are still holding on to their childhood desires and instincts.

They only take action on what they believe is best, even if the facts show that it isn't. Emotionally immature people also make decisions based on what feels good at that particular moment.

Check out this scenario which perfectly portrays this behavior. Mary persuaded her sister, Jane, to come to speak to their mother about some of the unhealthy habits she had picked up recently. Once they arrived and had spent some time with their mother, the moment came for them to begin the conversation. But Mary looked around and found out that her sister Jane was nowhere in sight. She looked all around only to see her getting into a cab and heading home. Mary was shocked as to why Jane would leave without any prior warning. However, to Jane, leaving was a better option than dealing with the uncomfortable and hard confrontation with their mother.

This is an example of how emotionally immature individuals pick situations that feel like the best one to them.

They are unable to deal with Stress properly

People who are not emotionally mature have problems dealing with stress the right way. Rather than taking a look at what is happening and thinking of a solution, they instead distort, deny, or change reality into something more suitable for them.

These individuals find it challenging to take accountability for their actions and instead blame others. They find it hard to keep their emotions in check and over-react to seemingly minor situations. These individuals don't understand how the internal scale for measuring their feelings works, which makes it impossible for them to control their outbursts. All of these make it impossible for them to care for anyone in the right manner.

As parents, their kids are the ones who suffer most of the blame when things go wrong, even when they are not at fault.

They are irritated by others with different perspectives

As we have covered earlier, emotionally immature people are incredibly rigid. It becomes much worse when others have perspectives or opinions that are different from theirs. They hate this and tend to get angry when others don't share the same views they do.

These individuals believe that others are meant to see things the way they do. It is also difficult for them to understand that it is normal for other people to have their own views. Even, they easily offend other people because they do not have proper knowledge of how every individual is unique. However, they are more likely to excel in relationships or situations where all the individuals involved have similar beliefs.

They don't make decisions with facts

Emotionally immature people do not analyze situations using facts. Instead of this, they go with their feelings when dealing with situations. This is the case even when what they feel is not true.

If you try to make these individuals see things using the evidence available, you won't make any headway. What they feel takes precedence over every other thing.

They are self-involved

Unhealthy self-involvement is typical of individuals dealing with emotional immaturity. They are always on the lookout to determine if someone has upset them. How they feel is dependent on how others react to them, and this is not normal behavior. If they get a good reaction, their self-esteem rises, and if the response is not what they require, it falls. This is different for emotionally mature people who don't need the reaction of others to feel great about themselves.

Since they are incredibly self-involved, they do not care about the needs of others. As parents, their needs take priority over those of their kids, who are left to fend for themselves.

However, for many of these individuals, this self-involvement may arise from the problems they had during childhood. These problems may have resulted in them having doubts about themselves as people. In essence, their self-involvement may not be like that of someone full of himself, but more like someone unable to help acting the way they do.

They Are self-centered

It's no news that emotionally immature people hold on to their childish behaviors. One of these is self-centeredness, which is common among children.

However, as opposed to children who are self-centered due to instinct, emotionally immature individuals do so because they are insecure. Children are innocent because they know no better and don't do it as a result of any malice. Emotional immature individuals remain insecure all their lives and use this behavior as a way of keeping all those areas they feel they lack hidden. This is also another reason they don't allow anyone to get close to them on an emotional level.

If these individuals do not get their needs met, they always lash out by throwing tantrums. Emotionally mature individuals can calm down and adequately express their desires without the need to lash out and act violently. But when it comes to emotionally immature individuals, the reverse is the case. And after they have lashed out, they refuse to be accountable or to apologize for their actions.

Still, these individuals may not even be aware that they are suffering from insecurities, and this makes their situation even worse.

They like to refer to themselves

People who are emotionally immature love to refer to themselves at all times. This applies even during conversations with others. Even when it is not necessary, they redirect conversations to their own experiences.

An example of this is a daughter telling her mother about how her day went, only for her mother to redirect the conversation to how terrible her day was. Another example would be a friend telling her close friend about her relationship problems, only for this friend to divert the conversation to one of her past relationships instead.

Even when they do manage to listen to you without interruption, their interests may lie elsewhere. And they won't ask questions that will help the conversation move forward and instead will use sentences that lead to the conversation ending quickly. For example, they may say something like, "I am so sorry, dear. It gets better with time."

What's more, these individuals don't self-reflect. For this reason, they are unable to look at the role they played in causing an issue and determine where they went wrong. If they were responsible for a problem, it is hard for you to hold it against them because they can easily dismiss it by letting you know they meant to harm.

They like to be the center of attention

Emotionally immature individuals enjoy being the center of attention. This is similar to children, but it manifests differently in these individuals. Emotionally immature individuals are not able to function properly until they are in a place where everyone appreciates them. This means everyone needs always to be focused on them, loving them, and satisfying their every need.

Emotionally Immature Parents

In any gathering, the person who has the least level of emotional maturity takes a considerable part of the energy and time in that gathering. If they are given a chance, they will take up all of the attention, and it is usually tough to get the focus back from them. This can go on unless there are people in the gathering who are willing to chip in their statements forcefully. However, this fails to happen most times as it is considered rude behavior, and not many people are eager to adopt it.

If these individuals are unable to get the attention they crave, or they lose it, they will do everything they can to get it back. This may mean throwing tantrums, sulking, withholding, engaging in dramatic activities, and so on.

As parents, these theatrics can have a ripple effect on their children. This could come in the form of shame, embarrassment, or sometimes guilt. Many of these kids will also believe that they don't deserve to be the center of attention themselves. Sometimes, these children take this feeling into adulthood. Also, because these individuals are unable to reflect on their actions, they may never believe their actions are affecting others negatively.

You need to remember that these individuals are not to be confused with extroverts. Although extroverts enjoy being out there and getting attention, they don't do it to eclipse everybody. Instead, they do it because they enjoy interacting with others and are more than happy when others chip into their conversations too. This is utterly different from emotionally immature individuals who do it because they want all of the attention on them at all times.

They encourage the reversal of roles

This is typical among emotionally immature individuals. However, it becomes more prominent when they become parents. Here, the parents treat their children like adults, and instead of being parents to them, the kids are conditioned to play the role of parents. They may treat them as therapists by bombarding them with their adult problems and expecting the child to understand.

For instance, John's mother was a single mother who lost her husband years earlier. Every day when she gets back from work, she informs John of the trouble she has at work alongside how difficult it is for her to raise funds and care for the home. She also lets him in on how tedious it has been for her to get a man to love her as a single mother.

All of these would have been great information to share with another adult who could have easily comprehended the situation. However, for thirteen-year-old John, this was too much, and he did not even know how to process all of this information. The result of this was a young boy saddled with adult problems he could not fix, which were starting to affect other areas of his life. In all of these, his mother expected him to console her and listen to her worries, not realizing the damage she was causing to him.

In other instances, the parent may expect their kids to be happy for them and shower them with praises instead of the other way around.

For example, Nancy's mother got tired of her marriage and without any warning, left Nancy with the responsibility of caring for her young siblings and her father. Of course, being a teenager, this was a complicated situation to deal with as she soon started playing the role of mother in the home. With time, she had almost no life of her own and started living a life no teenager would love.

Some years later, her mum came over with her new husband to take Nancy and her siblings for a visit to her new mansion. She expected Nancy to be excited and happy for her regarding all she had accomplished, but she never considered how difficult Nancy had it during her absence.

This is a perfect example of a role reversal in which a parent expects her kid to share excitement for her achievement.

They do not have empathy

For anyone who wants to establish a genuine emotional connection with others, having empathy is crucial. It is impossible to develop deep relationships without understanding. Because emotionally immature individuals are unable to get in touch with their feelings, they are unable to see how their behavior affects others.

Empathy involves being aware of the intentions and emotions of other individuals. For anyone who wants to have proper empathy, they need to be great at imagining what others are feeling. This way, you can understand the perspectives of other individuals because you know their thought patterns are not the same as yours.

Great emotionally mature parents have empathy and have the interests and needs of their children at hand. For parents to be able to imagine the feelings of their children properly, they need to be in tune with their own emotions too. This is not the case for emotionally immature parents, and this makes it impossible for them to determine how their children and others may be feeling.

In most situations, the emotionally immature parent reacts in a manner that may seem abnormal to other healthy people.

For instance, you are heading out at night, and they are worried about you getting kidnapped or killed. You are planning to get married, and they are extremely concerned about you leaving them. They are more concerned about expressing the emotion that initially arises, without being bothered about the way those around them feel.

They love controlling others

An immature person does not believe that anything should be outside his control. As long as all accept their ideas or behavior, they are fine. They want the world to be exactly the way they want it, others to behave how they want.

Most of the signals of underdevelopment in emotions are beyond the control of immature people. It's so bad that most parents who are very naive don't recognize it. What's even worse is that it always hurts their kids. The point of this chapter is not to heap blames on immature parents but to make you as a reader to understand why there are such parents.

Luckily, as grown-ups, we acquire the capability and freedom to evaluate whether our fathers and mothers will be able to give us the attention and kindness we yearn for. To actually review this accurately, it's significant to realize not only your fathers' and mothers' shallow traits but also their core emotional background. The moment you really get these behavioral patterns of your parents, that is when you begin to value or study things to expect from your father or mother, so then you can list down their traits, and their limits will not trap you. Make sure you have one thing in mind, though, that your fathers or mothers are private people. Right now, they don't know you've been doing your research as to why they are so aloof, but that's the point, they don't need to know. As you read through, also note that this book is especially useful for both parties: parents and children. The aim is of this book is so that you can expand the self-assurance that emanates from your story. Don't feel bad if you are a child, and you've ordered this book; you've done nothing wrong, and it doesn't mean you are trying to see your parents in a bad light. But it will teach you to know them more and learn a thing or two about yourself as a person.

Emotionally undeveloped parents may hurt their children's emotional growth and the relationships they will have when they become adults. These adverse effects usually stem from minor to severe. Still, it all depends on the parent's level of emotional immaturity, and also, the result is similar to children that feel lonely.

Behavioral Pattern Vs. Temporary Emotional Relapse

There's a difference between a behavioral pattern and something that is just a temporary emotional problem. Any person can momentarily lose emotional guidance or be abrupt when exhausted or stressed. A lot of us have so much to feel ashamed of when we think of some things we did back in time. However, if someone has behavioral patterns of emotional underdevelopment, such an attitude will likely show up constantly. These personalities are so involuntary that most people don't even know they are doing them. Emotionally underdeveloped people will never think back to their behavior and see what it does to people around them. Unlike normal people who think again and feel embarrassed about their attitude, they don't feel anything at all. They regret nothing.

Behavioral Patterns Connected With Emotional Underdevelopment

Emotionally Undeveloped people have a list of traits that you are going to learn as you read this chapter. Their personalities are interconnected, and they display various patterns and reactions to things. In the chapters that follow after this, you'll keep getting more things about parents with emotional immaturity and how to handle them.

Emotionally undeveloped people are very stiff And selfish

You must know that when people with an immature mind have a way around something, they'll go for it and even go as far as getting that goal without caring about people they stamp on in the way. Although, when they are in a relationship or make decisions that involve emotions, they become useless. It's not their fault, but they are so stiff or impetuous, and most times when they manage with things in life, they take the easy way around things.

Emotionally Immature People Can't Handle Stress

Another thing you should note about immature people is that they hate Stress. It's not something they can deal with so they freak out when they are under pressure. Now, imagine a parent who can't handle stress. How do you think they will be parents? Immature people will never accept their wrong-doings. They would rather push the blame on to people around them. It's easier for them to do that, and you know why? The moment an emotionally immature person is under pressure, they get upset, and it becomes a lot of hard work for them to handle things, and they are always in need to be pampered every single time even when they are wrong.

Immature People Only Do What Soothes Them

Have you ever noticed how children throw tantrums? Okay, let me explain it this way: young children are always happy when they get what they want and unhappy – which leads to tantrums – when they don't get what they want. Did you notice I used two key emotions most humans feel? Happy and unhappy! Yes, children function based on their emotions alone. But you realize as we grow, things change for us, and we start to take charge of what we feel, and even if we can't control how we feel, we do not let that control us. But that's not the same with emotionally immature people. Immature people act out on what they are feeling; they never keep calm to handle things logically. Mature people think first then act, but it is never the same for immature people.

They Don't Know How To Respect Other People's Point Of View

People who have difficulty with their emotions are so immature that they get angry when people have their own ideas. They are terrible with arguments because they always end up fighting with the other party. They want people to see things their way and never have their own opinion. They get so comfortable in situations that they believe everyone must have the same beliefs, and such beliefs must correlate with theirs.

Emotionally Immature People Are Always Conceited

Regular kids are self-centered when they are very young, but this should disappear by the time they become adults if it doesn't, then they end up being arrogant or emotionally immature adults. However, children are absolutely different from adults who are conceited though. When adults are conceited, joy and honesty are always absent from them.

When someone is immature, they are likely to be selfish because they always make excuses for their failures by stating they are occupied with something. In fact, emotionally undeveloped people are fixated on something in a crazy way that is totally different from a child's way of obsession. Kids are deep-rooted in this perpetual state of uncertainty, being afraid that maybe soon their peers will see them as wrong, insufficient, or unlovable. But pause, though, before you begin to feel bad for your kids, you must know that their defenses work flawlessly to subdue their nervousness below so that an adult won't even notice.

People Who Are Emotionally Immature Always Reference Themselves

People who are not emotionally mature tend to have discussions that will always lead back to them. Do you get it? They never want to have discussions where they will not get the chance to tell the other person, "Like me." When emotionally immature people wish to have a debate, they want the focus to be on them. They are less concerned about what new things they might learn in a discussion. They just want it to center on them alone.

People who are not emotionally mature are not good with social skills, so even when they have a discussion, they are never polite, and they do not listen. Note that it doesn't mean these people openly change the debate, but they are never interested in your discussion. They won't even ask questions about your experience on the said topic; in fact, they might keep quiet or ask questions about something entirely different just to diffuse the discussion.

Now, do you wonder if there are a lot of emotionally undeveloped parents?

I'll tell you this now: Yes, many parents are not so mature with their emotions, and I know you must wonder how the hell they will raise kids. But before we keep making up questions, how about you ask yourself this: what led these emotionally immature parents to turn out like this? It's mostly because they shut down emotionally as kids. Their parents weren't there for them emotionally either, and the cycle continues, it becomes a loop

People Who Are Immature Emotionally Can Be Unpredictable And Conflicting

Many emotionally immature people don't have a well-formed personality. They have different parts of them that make up their personalities. I know you think that is the way humans should be, right? You think we should be complex, and I totally agree, but it's not healthy to have a contradictory personality. Humans are not some kind of vehicle where parts can be bought so it can work, so it's weird to have clumps of contradictory nature.

Although, I understand that this happens because they never conveyed their emotions as a child. So, they become adults that are often emotionally conflicting. Their traits are feebly organized and end up showing emotions that conflict. They are always in and out of their feelings, and they won't notice how inconsistent their feelings have become.

Emotionally immature people judge things through the physical and avoid using emotions. Parents who are emotionally undeveloped usually do a good job providing for everything physical their children might need. They buy clothes, pay their bills, provide food, etc. for their kids, but they will never go further than that. When it comes to physical needs, they make sure they provide everything that will help their children.

These needs will be granted to their kids so far as it is something they can provide with their money and in their own capacity. That provision stops once it becomes an emotional need, and they just switch off without any explanation.

Some children will be taken care of when they fall ill and get their parent's attention, but this only happens when their parents are sure they are really sick. They were able to experience this care alone only after they were confirmed to be truly sick. It will likely be the only time such a child will receive any form of emotional connection with their parent.

Such immature people get confused with emotions. They don't even know what to do when it has to do with things that involve emotions, you can't blame them though, and they were likely never brought up by parents who gave them love or showed emotions. Such people follow the footsteps of their parents and so they only remember their parents ever being there for them physically. Although they also feel this pang of hurt for not been taken care of emotionally, they won't provide that to their kids because they don't know what it feels like to have an emotional bond with someone and they don't know how to achieve it

Emotionally immature people can be sadists

They dread genuine emotions, especially ones that express happiness, so to stop feeling this dread, emotionally immature people resort to ruining the moment. So when such people become parents, they will change the subject or warn their kids not to get their hopes up when their children are excited. Just to bring down their children's happiness and say something that shows unconcern.

People Who Are Immature Emotionally Are Also Shallow With Their Thinking

People who are not mature with their emotions can become overcome by emotions very quickly, and they show their nervousness by transforming such emotions. So rather than have deep feelings, they handle things and act sketchily. The way they react to things only indicates one thing, which is that they're zealous and very passionate, but the way they express their emotions mostly have oblique values.

Emotionally Immature Parents

Notes:

Emotionally Immature Parents

Chapter 3: Deep wounds left by Emotionally Immature parents

As you know, emotionally immature parents have some negative behaviors which can affect everyone around them. Even their kids are not left out.

Other people can easily choose to avoid hanging around these emotionally immature individuals, but the case is different for their kids. As children, we don't decide where we are born, and ideally, kids are meant to be raised by parents who have their interests in mind. Parents are the first people children come across, and they have a lot of influence on how these children turn out later in the future.

As kids, when we are sad or confused, the first people we contact are our parents. The same applies when we are sick or heartbroken. For many children, their parents are the safety nets that catch them when something beyond their control happens. This behavior may remain even as adults, and it is not necessarily a bad thing because this is how healthy parents should be.

These are the things we expect from our parents, and it can be such a letdown when our parents are emotionally immature. They don't protect you, neither do they make good safety nets. Reaching out to them for help is futile as they don't even know how to connect with you emotionally. All of these are only a few of the ways emotionally immature parents can affect the lives of their kids.

They Make Communication Impossible or Difficult

Under normal circumstances, communication is not an easy task. But it becomes much worse when dealing with a person who does not know how to connect or has terrible communication skills like an emotionally immature parent.

Many children who try to communicate with their emotionally immature parents are unable to make any headway. They find it difficult to connect and end up being shut down. As a child, this can be extremely frustrating in the long run.

They Make Their Children Angry

When kids are unable to connect or interact with their emotionally immature parents, it can bring about many emotions. As we stated above, frustration is one of these emotions. But it can also bring about the sadness of being unable to connect, and finally, it can bring about anger that their parents are not emotionally available.

Trying to connect with someone who is meant to protect you but instead dismisses you can build up anger inside you. This is an understandable response to this kind of scenario.

In other situations, children raised by immature parents are unable to express the anger they feel correctly. This may be because they know it is pointless to let it out, or it may only result in some form of abuse from their parents. The more they suppress this anger, the higher the possibility of dealing with other symptoms like self-blame and depression.

Some children develop habits like avoiding, lying, or forgetting as a way of expressing this anger they feel inside.

They Don't Try to Understand Emotions

Since emotionally immature parents are unable to connect on an emotional level, they cannot understand what others feel. This includes their children as well. Even when they are called out for the behavior, they react in a manner that states that they are not meant to try to understand how others feel.

Understanding the emotions of others is not easy, as it requires a lot of effort. You need to keep reading the other individual to decipher how they feel and how your behavior is affecting them. Ideally, parents are meant to put in this effort in understanding their kids. But this is the case only if they are emotionally mature.

Many emotionally mature people do all they can to ensure others are fine on the inside. They are willing to put in the work to ensure this because they will never be able to relax if they know they are leaving someone they love to deal with their issues alone.

Emotionally immature people, on the other hand, lack empathy and don't make any effort to understand emotions. They can easily ignore their kids since they have no empathy and couldn't care less.

They Make it Hard for Their Kids to Give to Them

People who are emotionally immature love being the center of attention and want everyone to focus on their needs. However, they don't make it easy for anyone to do this, especially their children. They want you to care and want you to be worried, but when you offer them help, they are not willing to take it. For example, if you suggest a solution that is certain to make them feel better, they refuse to accept it. They draw others in to help them but push them further when they make efforts to help.

They Expect Their Children to Mirror Them

Emotionally mature parents mirror their children as a way of showing empathy. This is usually unplanned and happens by instinct. They are sad and show concern when their kids are sad, and they are happy when their kids are happy too. This way, children feel safe and protected, knowing that their parents care for them.

However, this is not the case when it involves emotionally immature parents. Since they have no empathy, they are unable to mirror their children or understand them. In fact, they expect their kids to do this for them instead. They also find it extremely annoying when their children are unable to achieve this feat. These parents don't expect their children to have needs of their own and instead expect them to be what they want them to be.

Their Self-esteem Is Dependent on Their Kids

Emotionally immature individuals want to be the center of attention and have their needs met. Their self-esteem is at its peak when this happens and drops when it doesn't. They also apply this behavior when dealing with their children.

If they desire something from their kids and fail to get it, they can become distraught, and it can be a blow to their self-esteem. Since they don't expect their children to have personalities of their own, it is only fair that they try to work toward helping them achieve their every need.

Immature Parenting And Its Effects On Daily Life

In early and late childhood (6-12 years), parents mean the world to their kids. Children are entirely dependent on them for every little thing and want to hold on to them for support and care. Wounds at such a tender age may take years to heal, if not forever. The feelings of anger, neglect, and despair may linger through adulthood, and people often need external support for freeing themselves from the pain. The effect of immature parenting is visible in three main spheres of the child's life - daily activities, school / academic life, and social life.

The Tussles At Home

Immature parenting results in a childhood that is cut short. Children growing up with parents who are too involved in their own lives are often forced to take up responsibilities that they are too young for (example - cooking, watching out for siblings, doing other chores). And though many children grow up believing that sharing their parents' duties are making them more responsible, it actually does just the opposite.

The Storms At School

Hitches like parents not showing up in parent-teacher meets, or not giving enough attention to their kids' academic progress are common for children with less involved and detached parents. In many instances, these children get bullied by friends at school and they choose to get into a cocoon to save themselves from the everyday humiliations. And the result? Besides self-isolation and social phobia, such bitter experiences are capable of making them impulsive and resistant to positive thinking.

The Social Trauma

Have you ever been shamed because of your parents?

The social hazards are the worst part of the drama. Without any fault, children often become the soft targets of friends, family, and neighbors. They unknowingly become a part of what their parents do, and they may not have their parents by their side to help them fight this stress. The bruises of childhood may heal with time, and yes, it mostly does. But the effect of immature parenting stays inside and shows up in unexpected ways, which is why we must step up to soothe the wound so that the offspring don't have to deal with the same thing we did.

Emotionally Immature Parents

Notes:

Emotionally Immature Parents

Chapter 4: How Emotional wound passed on through Family Ties

Family ties spread emotional wounds, almost pitilessly. They look like a shade masked with words in the emptiness, looks, silences, and methods of rearing children. The emotional wounds can spread from one person to another in the family until it reaches to a person who has had enough and ends that process.

I know many of us have tried throwing a stone on the surface of a river or lake. When the stone hits the water surface, it creates a disturbance as it sinks into the bottom. The disturbance causes wavefronts.

The harder the impact, the more waves will be produced. It's like a silent scream's echo, an emotional wound's metaphor, and this influences a family member, and through him, the future descendants will have it too.

Families are secretive and very mysterious, and only a few areas, if any, exceed them. Many things happen in a family, and many of the happenings are transferred to the next generations of family members.

Just like the waves caused by a stone, a person's wounds can have a significant influence on other members of the family, just like waves eroding rocks on a beach or a puppet being moved by strings.

Emotionally Immature Parents

When talking on the source of emotional wounds, the common thoughts we have include tragically losing a loved one, physical violence, or sexual abuse. What we most of us do not know is that there exist emotional lacerations brought about by different dynamics.

Growing up in an environment that is not secure will undoubtedly cause emotional wounds. A person growing in such an environment will have many emotional wounds that will, most likely, be transferred to another person within the family.

Another trigger is when a person is in a family where it common having anger. In such a family, there is ungratefulness, reproach each other, emotional toxicity, and being undervalued continually are common.

Untreated chronic depression in the father or mother can also significantly impact the wounds. Established dynamics between children and their guardians, lines of communication, and defenselessness create scars that last for a lifetime.

Notes:

Chapter 5: Analyzing (or screening) types of Emotionally Immature Parents

You need to remember that some parents may be a combination of all kinds. This is understandable as many parents who fall into one of the categories tend to showcase other traits depending on the circumstance.

Some parents may also be narcissists, and the severity may differ. Also, some parents may add abuse to the mix. This could be sexual or physical abuse.

However, even if a parent in one category has a way of showcasing the traits you will find in another category, each one has its own significant flaws. Knowing these, let us take a look at these categories of parents below:

The Emotional Parent

Of all the types of parents, these are the most childish. These parents give everyone around them the impression that they are fragile and need all their care and attention. They get upset about insignificant things, and it will require a lot of attention from those around to appease them.

The kids of these kinds of parents are conditioned to deal with any feelings their parents exhibit at a particular moment. These children experience anger, sadness, and any other thing the parent may be feeling at some point. This kind of parent is emotionally imbalanced, and everyone around them learns to be careful when dealing with them, so they don't get upset.

Parents in this category with less severe conditions may only have mood swings. The children are left to deal with their constantly changing moods, which could go from high and low at any moment. This is usually unpredictable and can be very tasking for anyone around them.

In more severe cases, these parents could also battle with mental illness, personality disorders, or narcissism. In some cases, these kinds of parents may physically attack others around them when they are upset. It may also trigger them to cause harm to themselves via suicide attempts. Parents with this form of the severe case can get upset over the most insignificant reasons, and it could trigger the above behaviors. Their children are mostly at the receiving end of everything and quickly learn to do all of their parents bidding so they don't get angry and unleash their wrath.

For those who threaten to commit suicide, the children are placed in a more complicated situation because they don't even know what to do. The worst part is that it is something that can arise at any time, and these children learn to be on alert, caring for their parents, and ignoring their own needs in the process.

Whether a mild or severe case, these parents are not able to deal with stress the right way. Typical adults can manage stress and react appropriately, but for these parents, everything is difficult to handle. Furthermore, since these parents are unable to express themselves verbally, they use emotional manipulation to get their way from others. They hold grudges and keep tabs when they feel they have been offended and would like payback regardless of how long it takes. In even more severe cases, substance abuse comes into play, and this results in a parent who is unable to deal with a minimal level of stress and has an extremely volatile personality.

When outside, these parents can act and behave as normal parents should. However, in the home, everyone has learned to adapt to their every mood, and the mood in the house is always what these parents are feeling at that point. Children who are raised by these kinds of parents may learn to care for the needs of others while ignoring their own. This is something that can go on even until adulthood because that is how they were raised.

Check out this story that perfectly illustrates this type of parent:

John was used to catering to his mother's every need. However, he was able to get this under control as soon as he started a family of his own. This did not stop his mother from trying to manipulate him with emotions continuously. She always called John to get his attention and cater to her at every point. One day, John had enough and told her to stop calling as he was in a meeting. Still, she kept on calling anyway, and when he still refused to pick up, she sent a message threatening to kill herself.

Obviously, John was worried and went to find his mother. When he called her out on her behavior, she said, "I was only worried something had happened to you!" But the truth is she knew where he was and wasn't concerned about what he needed. Her priorities at that point were her desires, and that was to see and talk to her son, John.

The High-achieving Parents

In comparison to most of the other types of parents suffering from emotional immaturity, these types seem reasonable. These parents seem to have the interest of their kids in mind, especially when it comes to what they achieve and how successful they are. This makes it extremely difficult to notice that they are self-centered at the core.

In most cases, these parents who seem like high achievers, raise children who have problems with self-control or battle with depression. But these parents uniquely show their emotional immaturity. They believe everyone should value the same things they do and feel they know the best choice for others, including their children. Rather than believing their kids have a path of their own in life and accepting them, they urge them towards the direction they desire. Also, because they are very particular about achieving goals, they give it priority over everything else, including the way their children feel.

Many of these parents were raised in environments where they had no support emotionally. They grew up doing things by themselves without direction from anyone. They take pride in their independence and often make something good of themselves on their own. This makes them force the spirit of high-achievement onto their kids because they don't want to be embarrassed if their children don't succeed.

The children of these parents feel assessed continuously. A perfect example of this is a mother who makes her daughter practice her ballet steps in her presence so she can point out any errors. As a result of this kind of behavior, many of these children hate asking an adult for help with a problem.

And when they grow into adulthood, they continue with this behavior and may never ask those who are more experienced for any help. There are instances where parents in this category do odd things because they believe their way of doing things is the best. An example of this is a mother insisting on helping her son choose a new home because she thinks he would be unable to do it correctly.

Parents who are driven are often oblivious to the needs of their children. Their interests and desires don't matter, and they instead enforce their definition of what is right on their kids. The result of this for children of these parents is that they believe whatever they are doing is not enough.

The scenarios below are perfect illustrations of these parents:

Paul loved to sing, but his parents always felt he could do something better with his life. The only time he thought he had any control over his choices was when he was far away from them. Right from when he could remember, all his decisions have never been the correct one. Only what his parents decided was the best for him was acceptable.

Now, as an adult, he no longer has any idea of what his actual desires are. All he wants is to ensure his parents stay happy, and for this reason, he does anything they decide is best for him. Even when he went with the career path they chose for him, they always urged him to add a little extra effort, reminding him of how he had the potential to be one of the best in his field.

Looking at this from their perspective, they were only after the best for their son. However, they failed to see Paul as a human with his own personality and choices. They also failed to realize the damage they were causing to their son instead.

Now, Paul does not bother about setting any goals because it will only make his parents tell him how he could have done it better.

Another good example:

Mark is a doctor and a son to one of the best surgeons in the country, who was always on his case for him to be successful too. His father still controlled him and was easily irritated when Mark did not agree with his views. His father managed his entire life because he was trying to ensure that Mark was as successful as he was. Mark did not want to fail his father and tried to make his choices based on what his father would want. He was initially interested in accounting, but he knew his father would not approve and decided to go into the field of medicine instead.

His father almost had complete control of everything Mark did as he had grown to understand that standing his ground was pointless. Also, Mark's father had no empathy, which made him unable to see what was scary to his children. This made his teaching a terrifying activity for Mark.

When he wanted to teach Mark how to ride a bike, he took him up a slope, placed him on the bike, and left him. He did not provide any assistance or help but only said ride the bike. All of these did ensure that Mark excelled in his field, at least to others around him. But inside, Mark felt like he had no control of his life and that he was only a vessel being navigated by his father.

The Passive Parent

Just like the name states, these parents are less invasive and angry in comparison to the other types of emotionally immature parents. However, they hurt their children.

As opposed to the other kind of parents, these parents share emotional connections with their kids, at least to a reasonable extent. The instant things get too serious, they become passive and do nothing. These parents may love their children but won't have the capacity to offer them insights on ways to survive in the harsh world.

These parents can show empathy for their kids in comparison to others. They are also more playful and less complicated, even though they are not mature. However, if the needs of their children cross paths with their desires, they can withdraw the affection and empathy they show.

The passive parents may also use their kids to meet any emotional requirements they have. This could be by being the center of someone else's affection. They can come down to the level of their kids and interact with them, just like a kid would. The kids enjoy spending these moments with passive parents, but this becomes a form of an unhealthy relationship because the parent is only using the child to get the focused attention they desire. The relationship the passive parent shares with their kids can be downright uncomfortable to the extent of making the other parent jealous.

Even though the children of passive parents have fun with them and make them happy, the children quickly learn that they can't turn to these parents when they need them the most. Many of these parents are known to leave their children to defend themselves in toxic situations, especially when it involves the family. When the father is a passive parent, he may remain with a narcissistic partner who continuously abuses her kids emotionally and physically because he doesn't want the relationship to end. These kinds of fathers pretend not to know what is going on around them and can sometimes make excuses for the behavior of their partners.

For instance, after his mother violently attacked John, he went to his father for help, and his father brushed it off by saying, "Mum was only having a bad day. She only wants the best for you!"

As kids, passive parents learned to keep themselves below the radar and submit to those with much stronger personalities. This behavior remained with them as adults who did not realize they were meant to protect their kids. Rather than stand up for their kids when the kids bullied or abused, they instead go back into their shells as a way of dealing with the situation.

What's more, if these parents find a means to live a life that is much happier than they have presently, they may leave the family without a second thought. If this happens, the child of the passive parent finds it the most difficult because the passive parent is usually the one they love more.

Children who loved their passive parents are also affected when they become adults too. The love remains because they believe that their passive parents who had a real love for them just did not have the power to stand up for them even if they wanted to. These kids, as adults, grow to make excuses for others who portray the same behavior as their passive parents.

An example of this is stated below:

Mary had a father who was physically and verbally abusive at all times. Her mother was a stay at home mother without a job who showed her so much love and affection. For Mary, the best moments were those she spent around her mum. But anytime her father came back from work, she was always walking on eggshells and believed her mother was too.

Her mother spent most of her time in the kitchen cleaning or cooking when her father was home. She had no option to spend time with her father and was always given a good dose of physical and emotional abuse at the slightest error. She knew her mother could hear her scream and cry for help anytime this happened, but she never came to her rescue, and neither did she expect her to. In her mind, she felt her mother was helpless too and adored and respected her still.

Even when her mother was present anytime the abuse began, her typical reaction was to head to another part of the home to get "busy."

The Rebuffing/Rejecting Parent

These parents have the least amount of empathy among all of the parents we have covered. To their children, the rejecting parents seem to be in a castle of their own with massive doors keeping everyone out. They don't enjoy hanging around their kids or anyone else and seem happiest when no one bothers them.

Because of the way they act, their children feel they are not wanted. They also think that it would be best if they were not in the picture. Kids of these types of parents quickly learn that they should not go to them for help with anything. If you try to interact emotionally with them, they push you away, and if you keep trying, these parents can become outraged. And when angry, they are capable of physically abusing their kids.

The rejecting parents also have no empathy, and their favorite way of letting others know their presence isn't wanted is to adopt an unfriendly look or blank stare. Fathers are very common as rejecting parents. For example, a father who everyone in the home knows never to upset and who has no emotional connection with his kids may be a rejecting parent.

Kids who were raised in homes with these parents grow to believe no one wants to be irritated by them. Due to this, they try not to complain or to ask consistently when they need something. As adults, this can be very damaging as they won't understand how to push when asking for something they need.

For example, Racheal's father never wanted to talk to her or show affection like typical parents did. Sometimes, Racheal wondered if he was her father because he was quick to dismiss her whenever she tried to interact with him or spend time around him.

Even as an adult, her father was never open to speaking for too long on the phone and was quick to end conversations. To Racheal, her father was just an icon in her life she learned to stay away from.

Emotionally Immature Parents

Notes:

Chapter 6: Children born Adult: Different Children reactions

Children who are brought up by emotionally immature parents react differently to their experiences. Some of them adopt different coping mechanisms which they use in dealing with the things they have been through.

Some of them imagine instances of how the situation may change later down the road and how their parents will offer them the love and affection they desire. However, this hardly ever happens. Others cope by creating a role for themselves in the family to get attention from their parents.

None of the coping methods these children adopt allows them to heal fully or give them the feeling they desire.

Why Children Dream up Fantasies

When a child has an emotionally immature parent, they learn to adjust to the needs of their parents. To interact with their parents and get the care they desire, children may react in different manners.

However, the prevalent method children use to cope is to dream up fantasies about how everything will be fine in the long run. They may imagine that their parents will become the type they desire later in the future. This is a typical method children use to feel better by dreaming up stories about scenarios that will bring them true happiness later on.

For this reason, most people who dream up fantasies start with, "If only." For example, people may believe that their parents would love them and show them the affection they crave if only they could attain success. Others may think that if they do everything their parents want them to do, their parents may change into better ones. For others, they may believe that their lives may become better if only they found a partner with a specific character trait.

This is usually the way it goes. However, the sad news is that this is a solution that is crafted from the mind of children. In real life, especially as an adult, it is not a solution that works.

Still, this is the way numerous individuals deal with all the pain that came their way as children. They dream that everything will be alright in the future and that they would get the love they desire to help them make it through these perilous times.

How Do These Made-up Dreams Affect Relationships as Adults?

For many kids who have fantasies and dreams, a way of expecting them to come true is to leverage their relationships. They might believe that if they can keep up with these dreams, people are going to change with time.

Many of them may think that the emotional void they have will be sorted out by a perfect partner. Or it may be filled if they become who someone wants them to be. However, many of these dreams and fantasies tend to have the opposite effect. For instance, Joanne believed that she could only be happy if she could make her depressed mother happy. She didn't realize that her happiness was not dependent on anyone, even her mother.

In another example, Mark felt he could get his mother to love him the way he wanted if he did everything to please her. When he realized that nothing was changing even with all the effort he was putting in, he got angry. This is because he had been building this fantasy right from when he was a kid and hoped that by being self-sacrificing, everything was going to be alright.

Those trying to find their fantasies in others don't usually see how unrealistic it is. But a third party can notice it, which is why therapy is always an excellent option for getting past this.

How Does a Role-self Come into Play?

The moment children of emotionally immature parents realize that they are unable to get the attention they desire from their parents by being themselves, they develop a role self. This is more like an alternate self that they feel will help them get accepted in the family.

It is based on the conviction that if they attend to the feelings of others to the detriment of theirs, they would become accepted and loved with time. Some kids develop negative roles like truancy and other behaviors likely to get them the attention they desire.

How Is This Influenced by Parents?

A parent who urges a child to take up an activity they failed at when they were younger so they could tap from the success through this child is an excellent example of how a child influences role-self.

For kids who find themselves adopting the role-self given to them by their parents, the harder they realize it is to find their genuine self. With time, it diminishes as they make themselves more like individuals that their parents would accept.

However, playing a role-self is not sustainable because sooner or later, your true self will be unleashed. It can be exhausting to play the role of someone else instead of just being you. Pretending to be something you are not is quite tasking, and the fear of being exposed makes you unsettled.

Regardless of who you try to be, your real desires will crop up. The instant you can let go of these made-up roles and instead move toward your authentic self, you can live a much better life.

How Children Cope with Emotionally Immature Parents

Kids of emotionally immature parents cope with the lack of emotional connection by either internalizing or externalizing their problems. Internalizers are of the notion that it is their role to change circumstances. On the other hand, externalizers believe it is the role of someone else to do so.

Many children pick one of the two coping methods, but some leverage both methods. The goal of both ways is to achieve their needs, but the style selected is usually dependent on the personality of the child in question.

Nonetheless, the best option is to strike a balance between both coping methods. In this section, we will be taking a more in-depth look into both of these methods and what they entail.

Emotionally Immature Parents

Notes:

Chapter 7: Recognizing the problem awaking from the nightmare

Having understood how emotionally immature parents interact with their children, let us delve into the implications of these actions for their kids. Some of these can go on even until adulthood and affect every part of their lives, including how they relate with other individuals.

However, you need to understand that not everyone raised by an emotionally immature parent will have problems later as adults. Some adults make it a point to be much better parents and people than their emotionally immature parents.

They understand the toll it can have on a child and make it a point never to let their kids experience the same thing. Still, circumstances are not the same for everyone, and a good percentage of children of these parents face the consequences later down the line.

Inability to Keep Relationships

The things we go through as children have a way of affecting us in adulthood, and being raised by an emotionally immature parent is no exception. Kids who get the right amount of emotional support and love learn to have healthy relationships later on. When the reverse is the case, there are significant repercussions.

Children who were unable to get the right emotional support and guidance from their parents, and who dealt with abuse, will find it challenging to maintain relationships. Because of the treatment they faced from their parents; they may have developed traits to help protect themselves as adults like being extraordinarily protective and defensive.

This could result in numerous unstable relationships for this type of individual. It is mainly because these protective coping mechanisms can prevent a person from completely trusting those they get in a relationship with. In the end, they never enjoy the type of genuine happiness a loving relationship is supposed to bring, and this may cause frequent breakups.

The inability of these individuals to trust and let anyone can also affect other parts of their lives, aside from intimate relationships. Many of them are unable to interact with those around them appropriately, including co-workers, friends, and so on.

In worse cases, it prevents them from seeking the help they require to get better. Therapy is a great way to get treatment, but it requires a person to trust the expert completely and to let them in so they can get help. Since they are unable to achieve this feat, getting help can be an impossible task for many children of emotionally immature parents.

Furthermore, these adults tend to be scared of love and being attached to a person. The sad part is that they may be unaware that their traits are responsible for causing them issues in their relationships. For some, they start to push away anyone who seems to be getting too close to them since they have been raised to never let anyone in completely.

Self-centeredness

Similar to the emotionally immature parents who raised them, many of the children also grow into selfish and self-centered adults. This is understandable since they usually learn to fend for themselves at an early age. Many children grow into believing that there is no one to stand up for themselves, and this makes them give priority to their needs alone even if they have to blank out those of others

Lack of Self

As kids, our parents have a significant role to play in helping us determine who we are. This is something we learn from our parents, unconsciously and consciously. However, this is only possible when a parent lets you in and offers you guidance.

Emotionally immature parents are unable to do this and fail to play this role in the lives of their kids. In the end, the kids won't have an understanding of who they are, even when they grow into adults. As adults, these people don't know the path to take in life or what to do with their lives. Many of them end up in careers or marriages they never really wanted but came across while navigating the world blindly.

Even when the emotionally immature parent does seem to have little impact on helping their kids find their identity, it is usually what the parent feels is best. Most times, the kids grow into adults who end up doing everything they can to please their parents even in their life choices. They have no idea of the route to take in the first place, and so they do what their parents decide for them. Thus, even if they become successful in their respective fields, they are never really fulfilled on the inside since the person they have become isn't who they are.

Having a solid foundation when it involves forging your identity has a lot of impact on the kind of life you lead. Without knowing the person you are, you will be no different from a blind man trying to get past a busy road. Your only way through will be to allow someone to lead you through what he or she feels is the best course to take.

If you could see, you could have decided the best path for you instead of just following someone else. If you can't create your identity, you will follow just about anybody and let anyone who seems more grounded lead you through life. The course they decide to take may not always be the best option for you.

Substance Abuse

Children who consistently deal with shaming, physical and emotional abuse, and rejection from their parents, among others, tend to have a lot of anguish, pain, and anger stored inside. Like we stated earlier, they also learn while growing up that expressing what they feel is pointless and instead choose to keep all these feelings buried.

This may go on into their adult lives, and after some time, holding on to this pain becomes almost unbearable. Many of them choose to cope with all of these feelings by turning to substances to help them ease all they feel inside or take it away.

But substances provide only a short reprieve, and this means the cycle will have to be repeated anytime the effects of the drugs wear off. Doing this continuously becomes an addiction that makes the life of the person even worse.

Losing a parent is painful, but it is even worse when the parents are alive but are your source of pain and abuse and are unable to render help in any form. In worse situations, instead of abusing substances as a way to cope, the adult children of emotionally immature children may deal with depression and even suicidal thoughts. This usually occurs when the pain becomes too much for them to hold on to and deal with.

Problems Accepting Change and Understanding Emotions

Children raised by emotionally immature parents never learned how to deal with their emotions the right way. This is something healthy parents usually imbibe in their kids, but emotionally immature parents lack this capacity.

All of these could make it extremely difficult for these children to accept change. They would instead prefer things to stay the way they are, and if there is a change, they never know how to deal with it.

Furthermore, since these children never learn how to communicate their emotions, they are also unable to understand them. They may be unable to point out the things they feel or to let you in on it even if they want to. Also, they may be unable to understand the emotions of others, which may lead to a long streak of broken and short relationships.

Another ripple effect of not learning to communicate their emotions properly is that adults who had emotionally immature parents never learned how to create healthy boundaries. Due to this, these adults may try to recreate the relationship they had with their parents using other individuals they meet. This often results in these adults seeking romantic interests who can play the role their parents failed to. In the end, it can cause an imbalance in the relationship, making it end faster than it should have.

Low Self-esteem

As children, we depend on our parents to satisfy our emotional requirements while growing up. If there is no one to help us meet these needs, which is the case when emotionally immature parents are involved, it could lead to low self-esteem. This is a condition that may remain even when the children grow into adults.

However, this is not the only way a low-self-esteem may arise. Depending on the emotionally immature parents a child has, he or she may be rejected by their parents, or grow into believing that their efforts are not reasonable enough. For those raised by parents who refuse them, the children may see themselves as a mistake or unwanted.

The same also applies when a parent talks down to their kids when they make mistakes or makes them feel like disappointments because they refused to do what the parent wanted. All of these can have a significant impact on the self-esteem of these individuals who may grow into adults unable to stand up for themselves, who continuously shame themselves, and feel they are never going to be good enough.

Having low self-esteem may also affect other areas as well:

- As adults, these individuals are scared of rejection and can be very sensitive to it. The case remains the same if they feel they may be rejected, even when they haven't been denied yet. For example, an adult raised by emotionally immature parents, suffering from low self-esteem, may become distraught at the idea that someone they have an interest in did not like their proposal. This is a situation that a person with healthy self-esteem can easily handle and brush off since they already understand that rejection is a part of life. But for the children of emotionally immature parents, this is not the case.

•From the fear of rejection, perfectionism could also arise. Since these adults are worried about being rejected and can't handle it, they tend to become high achievers and have a huge desire to be accepted. These adults try to make everything they do perfect, and this could spill into other aspects of their lives, like their hobbies, relationships, and even their work. Since it is impossible to be perfect at everything, this could lead to many problems, especially with those involved in their lives.

They Tell Lies

These adults may also adopt lying as a means of expressing their feelings or getting the acceptance their parents never offered from others. They may lie to be who they are, not in a bit to get others to accept them or love them.

They Become Overcompensating Parents

Since many children of emotionally immature parents understand the pain it brings, they may make it a point to ensure their kids never face the same situation. This is not a bad idea, and many of them end up becoming good parents who have balanced relationships with their children.

However, for others, they may overdo it by becoming too involved in the lives of their children. Even though their intentions may be great, they may end up raising spoiled, narcissistic children who believe the world revolves around them. In other cases, their children may be unable to do anything on their own without the help of their parents because they get used to their parents handling and overseeing every area of their lives.

Chapter 8: Being an Internalizer

Internalizing children who are very perceptive will quickly notice when their parents are not connecting with them. A less aware child cannot register emotional hurt the way that perceptive internalizing children do and so are less deeply affected growing up with emotionally immature parents. Internalizers are sensitive to the subtleties of relationships and so are much aware of the loneliness that occurs as a result of emotionally unengaged parents.

Internalizers are Very Sensitive and Perceptive

Internalizers are very sensitive and do notice a lot of things far more than most people. They have been prompted to be attuned to other people's feelings and needs by their senses. This perceptiveness can be both a burden and a blessing. Internalizers could have had a vigilant nervous system from birth. Research has demonstrated that differences in babies' environmental attunement and perceptiveness can be observed at a very early age. This also dictated the kind of behavior exhibited by the children as they grow; this thus shows a possibility that a predisposition to a particular coping mechanism exists from early childhood.

Internalizers have Strong Emotions

Emotions of Internalizers tend to intensify because they are bottled in and not immediately released or acted out like in externalizers. Internalizers can often be seen as too emotional or just overly sensitive because they feel things deeply. They tend to cry when they experience something painful, and some parents just can't stand this due to being scared of emotional displays. Conversely, externalizers act out any strong feelings they experience before they can experience any internal distress. Most people will likely view the externalizer as having a behavioral problem instead of an emotional one while not being aware that emotions are the root of the problem.

Emotionally immature parents can punish externalizers for their behavior but will instead dismiss an internalizer's feelings with contempt. Internalizers are sometimes told that their very nature is their problem while the focus is placed on the behavior of the externalizer.

Internalizers Have a Deep Need for Connection

Internalizers are sensitive to the quality and genuineness of emotional intimacy in their relationships because they are attuned to feelings. They strongly desire emotional intimacy. Internalizers need to share their inner experiences; their desire for a real emotional connection is an excellent part of their existence. For internalizers, nothing hurts more than being around people who cannot engage them emotionally. It is not a social urge for them but rather a strong hunger to connect on a more intimate level with like-minded people who can understand them. When they are unable to make this kind of connection, they feel lonely emotionally.

When children who are internalizers have self-involved or emotionally unengaging parents, they do think that being helpful and neglecting their own needs will win their parent's love. However, being counted on does not equal being loved, and the emptiness of this strategy becomes apparent. Despite that, these children still believe that to make a connection, they need to put other people's needs before theirs and treat others as more important. They think that by being the giver in a relationship, they can sustain it, but they do not know that conditional behavior cannot get unconditional love.

Internalizers Have Strong Instincts for Genuine Engagement

Have you ever given thought to why feelings of disconnection and isolation are stressful? Is it that it is merely less pleasant to be alone, or maybe there is something more to it? Why is an emotional connection so crucial? It was not so surprising to know mammals can reduce the physical effects of stress by seeking contact with others. Stress hormones and heart rate can be reduced by comforting gestures such as touch, eye contact, soothing sounds, and physical closeness. These effects calm and also create social bonds.

Understanding That Connection is Normal, Not Dependent

Internalizers should view their instinctive desire for emotional connection as a positive thing, strength instead of as a negative, seeing it as being too dependent or needy. Turning to others for succor when stressed makes people more adaptive and stronger. These emotional needs show that their instinct for seeking comfort is healthy and functional. Instinctively, internalizers do know that there is strength in being interdependent, this could be seen in the popular saying: "strength in numbers." Seeing wanting understanding and empathy as a sign of weakness is characteristic of emotionally immature people.

Forging Emotional Bonds Outside of the Family

Children who are internalizers tend to find sources of emotional connection outside of the family because of their heightened perception and a strong need for emotional engagement. They are aware of when people respond to them warmly, and so they seek relationships with these people outside the family to have a greater sense of security. Internalizers can get emotional nourishment from resonating with art and nature. They can also embrace spirituality to give the emotional nurturing they strongly desire as they relate to a greater who is always with them.

Externalizers similarly have needs for emotional comfort, but they instead take other people emotionally hostage by forcing those needs on them. Most times, externalizers use their behavior to manipulate specific responses from people. Still, due to them achieving these responses through manipulation, it is not as fulfilling as a genuine exchange of intimacy. People who have been blamed or guilt-tripped by externalizers end up feeling forced to help, and this can lead to a build-up of resentment.

Relationship between Emotional Immaturity and Avoiding Engagement

Emotionally immature people are externalizers who are unable to reap the benefit of genuine emotional engagement and calm themselves. When experiencing bouts of insecurity, they feel threatened and stressed, and instead of seeking comfort from people launch into flight, fight, or freeze behaviors that are commonly observed in reptiles. They tend to react to anxious moments in their relationships by resorting to rigid, defensive behaviors that result in other people being alienated rather than being connected to. Externalizers have inadequate skills in reaching out to people for soothing and comfort, and they display domination, blame, anger, and criticism.

When externalizers get upset, it sometimes seems like they have a strong desire for emotional engagement, but this approach tends towards panicking instead of connecting. It requires a whole lot to make them calm, but despite that, they remain dissatisfied because of their inability to connect fully.

Physical Survival: The Role of Emotional Connection Skills

Having a strong drive for succor through genuine emotional connection has benefits that surpass merely making people feel better, it can save lives. Getting reassurance and support from close relationships can help people to survive extreme and life-threatening conditions. If fight, flee or freeze up behaviors are a person's only coping mechanism during stress, then it will be tough to endure a lengthy challenge. Research has shown that people who survived impossible situations lived through such circumstances by calling upon their existing relationships and the memories of those they love as a source of strength and will to survive. Everyone needs a sense of genuine intimate connection to feel entirely secure, and there is nothing wrong with that.

Internalizers are often Embarrassed about Needing Help

After finally seeking help, internalizers are mostly apologetic and feel undeserving of receiving such support. Internalizers, who grew up in a family with emotionally immature parents are often surprised when they find out that their feelings are being taken seriously. They downplay their emotional needs, and some even believe they shouldn't get therapy because there are people who need more help than they do; this indicates that they most likely grew in a home where externalizers were the only ones who were helped.

If shamed for showing their sensitive emotions as a child, when they become adults, they may become embarrassed to display any deep emotion. They can apologize for crying in a therapist's office when talking about their emotional problems. They are often convinced that displaying their deepest feelings means that they are inconveniencing other people. When people show genuine interest in the feelings of an internalizer, they often become surprised and are caught off-guard.

Internalizers Become Invisible and Easy to Neglect

Externalizers are very easy to spot in a family; they are the kids who get annoyed over the most straightforward matter, the teenagers who keep getting into trouble, and the adult children who cause nothing but problems. Externalizers are always at the top of their parents' concerns. Parents with externalizer children tend to devote more time and energy to them than to other children.

Internalizers, on the other hand, often appear to be getting on just fine and do not need much attention or nurturance as the externalizers because the internalizers instead rely on their own inner resources. Internalizers are often afraid to ask for help and often resort to solving their problems on their own. They are often low-maintenance kids who do not require much attention and are very easy to overlook. For preoccupied parents, self-reliance may precipitate emotional neglect.

Emotionally immature parents believe that their internalizing children can sufficiently take care of themselves and so they allow them to have an independent life outside of the family. Although internalizing children can be independent and cope successfully, they still desire to capture the interest of their parents and connect with them. No child deserves to be emotionally invisible and especially not highly emotionally attuned and sensitive internalizers.

Getting by on Limited Recognition

When growing, internalizers that are emotionally neglected continue to feel as if they have to do everything on their own, and then they become more adept at doing this. Internalizers can assimilate whatever they get from others because they like to learn and remember experiences. Internalizers also have an excellent emotional memory and will, and they reach within themselves when they are not getting emotional nurturance from others. Internalizers often take on so much responsibility for other people without much thought. They are so very grateful for even the tiniest bit of recognition, and this is one of the specific characteristics of an internalizer.

Recognizing Childhood Neglect

When parents are emotionally immature, it is guaranteed that their children will suffer emotional neglect. This deprivation, however, is silent and is an invisible experience for these children, they will feel emptiness, but they will not know what name to ascribe to it. They will grow up like this and still not be able to identify or realize that they are suffering from emotional loneliness, but they will feel different from those who truly seem at ease.

People often do not realize that they are suffering from or have suffered emotional deprivation until they read about it for the first time. The self-sufficiency of children who are internalizers often creates the impression that they have no needs. They are expected to be okay without anyone looking out for them or carefully watching over them. They are often referred to as "old souls," and their parents trust them always to do the right things.

Learning to Ignore One's Feelings and Receiving Only Superficial Support

When children have had to become tough and learn to do things on their own, they can develop an attitude of rejection towards their own feelings. They have likely learned to keep away from those painful feelings which their emotionally immature parents cannot help them with.

Neglect can also occur in the form of emotionally immature parents giving such comforts that do not really help the scared child in any way.

Internalizers are Overly Independent

Emotional neglect can make premature independence to seem like a virtue. A lot of people who suffered emotional neglect as children do not often realize that their independence was not a choice but a necessity. Independent children may not learn how to seek help when they grow up even when such support is readily available. Psychotherapists and other counselors have the responsibility of coaxing these people to accept help by making them see that their need for help is legitimate.

Internalizers do not See Abuse for what it is

Internalizers are unable to recognize abuse for what it is because they look within themselves when things go wrong to seek for the reasons that something went wrong. If parents do not see their actions as abuse, the child won't recognize it as such either. As adults, internalizers still do not have any idea that they had been abused in their childhood. As a result, they even do not recognize abusive behavior in their adult relationships.

Internalizers do Most of the Emotional Work in their Relationships

It is not surprising that internalizers put in a lot of emotional work into their relationships. Emotional work includes using self-control, empathy, and foresight to get along with others and to foster relationships. Parents do most of the emotional work in healthy families. Still, when the parents are unable to cope, an internalizing child will step into the gap created by such parents, and such a child can become overly responsible.

Adapting Compensatory Cheerfulness

Internalizing children can take up a cheerful role to bring liveliness and happiness, especially when parents are depressed, into a melancholic family climate. With their excellent sense of humor and liveliness, they try to help others to feel that things are not as bad as they seem.

Doing Emotional Work for Parents

Emotionally immature parents will avoid emotional work at any opportunity they get and so may not deal with their children's emotional issues or attention problems, thus leaving the children to work through it on their own. Emotionally immature parents are unhelpful when their children need emotional support; they may be dismissive when their child expresses his feelings of being hurt. Internalizers, due to their natural sensitivity, do emotional work for their parents, and sometimes, internalizers play the role of emotional support before they are old enough to do so.

Overworking in Adult Relationships

Internalizers are used to supplying most of the empathy in their relationships, and they often believe that they can be able to love someone into a good relationship single-handedly. Since they do most of the work in trying to get along with people, they become worn out without noticing that the other person is not changing at all. Internalizers are so used to providing the sensitivity missing in their family members, and they automatically do this with everyone. They sometimes take up emotional slack in their relationships by playing both parts of the interactions and act as if there is reciprocity when, in fact, there is none.

Internalizers often end up in unequal relationships despite doing their share of the emotional because needy externalizers are more likely to go after warm and giving internalizers, they can initially make the internalizer feel special to secure the relationship, and when that has been accomplished, they stop reciprocating. The internalizer, however, believes that they are to blame for this change in the relationship.

Attracting Needy People

Emotionally immature people cannot resist relying on self-contained internalizers because these internalizers seem so strong and do not require help or support from anyone else. Internalizers are perceptive and sensible, and this makes even people that they have met before trusting them. Needy strangers will take up a sensitive person's time and attention at the slightest chance they get.

Internalizers are extremely sensitive and very perceptive of other people's needs. Growing up with emotionally immature parents is very painful for Internalizers because of their strong desire to connect emotionally with someone. Internalizers are prone to be emotionally neglected by emotionally immature parents because they refrain from bothering other people with their "strong" emotions. They create a healing fantasy that makes them believe that they can change other people's behavior and feelings about them while also developing a role-self that's totally focused on other people. Internalizers do a lot of emotional work in their relations and even end up doing too much while they can get by on very little support from other people. When internalizers do too much emotional work in their relationships, they can become exhausted and even start to harbor resentment.

Emotionally Immature Parents

Notes:

Emotionally Immature Parents

Chapter 9: Dealing with Emotionally Immature Parents Aging

When we were children, we had so much confidence in our parents that we saw them as semi-god. You can blame it on childhood because we believed they could never be wrong. The more we grow, from the stages of adolescence to adulthood, we know better, but this belief is not permanently eradicated. All of these occur due to beliefs and some things we have been made to believe even when the contrary is occurring in our presence.

Some of the beliefs include:

- Only your parents genuinely want the best for you

- Even when you trust no one, your parents should be an exception.

- Your parents love you

- Parents are wiser

- They will always be there for you

- You can trust their advice

Everything they tell you is true

All of these are true as parents are amazing, but when your parents are immature, then all of the statements cannot work for you. This chapter aims to help you know your parents and guidelines on how to relate with them without losing yourself in the process. There are unreal beliefs that a parent will change.

The Unreal Belief That A Parent Will Change

When children feel unloved by their parents, they feel incomplete and do all they can to make them have a change of mind. But in most cases, the anger they vent on the children is not due to the way they act, as children are lovely, but rather it can be the circumstances that surrounded their birth, or they want to make up for their own childhood hurt. When you view it from this aspect, you will agree with me that changing their heart is a lifetime fantasy.

On the verge of trying to gain their parent's heart, children go as far as hopping around them and trying to please them at any given opportunity. This zeal isn't curbed by adulthood, rather, they keep hoping and trying their best.

Isolated Observation

Checking out everything you have read in this book, you already know how to identify immature parents. Think of your parent that falls into this category and act your own true self to them as its less probable that you will win them over as a loving parent.

Family system theory, which was proposed by Murray Bowen in 1978, gives an insight into how immature parents create emotional enmeshment over their children's true selves. Immature parents do not have genuine conversations and intimacy with their children. Such families are better referred to as housemates. Bowen further explained that when parents tend to cause emotional injuries to their children, rather than the children sitting to mourn, such children should indulge in other things that make them happy without losing themselves in the process.

Become Observational

You can only have a peaceful conversation with immature people when you allow yourself to feel calm and relaxed. So being observational is a practical act, not a theory. You can start by detaching your frame of mind and being observational rather than trying to prove a point because you might not win. Do not allow emotions to be in charge of your attitude towards them. Do not be bothered by what they say, instead think of something else, travel far and wide in your mind, and win yourself over instead of allowing them to disturb your heart.

When you discover you are already reacting to their words, detach your mind immediately and, in your mind, go over how that person has acted towards you in the past. That way, you will look at them as whom they really are without having to prove a point to them. From the moment you are feeling, you can't take it anymore; find a way to excuse yourself. Go to a place you can feel relaxed and distracted. Your observational acts will keep you strong and make you be yourself rather than the person people have defined you as.

The Maturity Awareness Approach

This approach helps you to consider the emotional maturity of others when you are dealing with them. You categorically estimate the maturity of the person you are dealing with in your head, and it gives you an insight into how you should relate with them.

You should deal with emotionally mature and immature people differently. Here is an aid on how to deal with people that you consider emotionally immature without hurting yourself.

*Communicate and let go: Express yourself calmly and politely and turn a deaf ear to the result

*Keep the relationship away and focus on the outcome: Be sure of the need for the conversation and don't be involved in a conversation that requires the changing of the mind of your parents. Let your

communication come with a goal that is feasible to be achieved.

•Cope and do not engage: The interaction should be precise, and the time should be well managed. Do not give room for emotional conversations that would hurt you.

Changing An Old Self Role

Your emotional freedom can only begin when you do not just consider your parent's maturity status but also examine your attitude if you are your true self or you play a role self. When you have seen where you play the role self, then you are a step ahead, and all that is required of you is to change your role and do what you feel is best for you.

Minding Your Feelings And Thoughts

When you can control your own thoughts and feelings, then it will be easier for you to interact with immature people. To do this, you have to begin by being observational; you should adopt the maturity awareness approach. With this act, you will develop immunity to whatever is thrown at you, and you will be calm even when blame is directed at you.

When you are dealing with parents, having predicted the outcome of the conversation will help you keep calm as you already have an idea of what their response would be.

Be Cautious Of Changes in People

According to Murray Bowen (1978), "as a child becomes more of an individual, the emotionally immature parent's knee-jerk reaction is to do something that attempts to force the child back into an enmeshed pattern. If the child doesn't take the bait, such parents may ultimately start relating more genuinely".

You need to be careful when your parents show unusual openness, especially when you just adopted your observational approach. Once they start doing the things you have been pleading with them to do, be careful not to get trapped or lured into being your old self. Keep tabs, and let's see how long it will last before you fall into the trap. Your inner mind would be glad that you have succeeded in winning the heart of your parents, but you should let them know you aren't changing your true self. If you fall back and trust their changes, you might be disappointed.

The truth is your parents will want to come closer when they feel you are drifting apart. When you operate from your renewed mind, you will keep the gap while they do the changing if it is genuine. Never forget to keep observing and be true to yourself. You shouldn't lose yourself for anything or anybody.

Tips To Deal With Immature Parents As An Adult

As an adult child of an immature parent, it is expected that you will feel anxious, worried, and outrageous at times when you see things going out of your control. And if this is what you are dealing with right now, here are some tips that can help you.

1. Separate spaces

Separate your time for your parents and your spouse and kids, when it gets challenging to find the right balance. Work on a plan, for example, you meet your parents on weekends and spend as much time with them as you can. Take your kids along with you, if that will make your mum and dad feel more loved.

2. Replace negative talk with a positive one

If your parents were unable to reflect your emotions since childhood, it is not your fault. Start believing in yourself no matter what. Avoid negative self-talk and make space for more gratitude, self-love, and positivity in life. Remind yourself that your childhood is over, and you are out of the trauma now.

How to replace negative self-talk with positive statements

Negative Talk	**Positive Talk**
1. I couldn't express myself to my family	1. I tried my best to explain. Couldn't have done anything more
2. I deserve to be punished	2. I deserve to be happy
3. I am not a good son/daughter	3. I am a good son/daughter
4. I have to sacrifice my happiness to make my parents happy	4. If my parents love me, they would never want me to sacrifice my happiness
5. I can't move out. I have to look after my mum and dad	5. My parents are my responsibility, but I can't take care of them unless I have a decent career
6. I should not raise my own family	6. I will settle down when I want to

3. Don't get emotionally stunted

Don't ever be at the giving end of what you had received from your parents in childhood. Show love to your family and try to empathize with them. Emotionally distancing yourself will make you end up being the same as your parents are.

4. Communicate as often you want

As a child, it may have been trying for you to find the right words for expressing yourself. But you are an adult now, and you should be in charge of your life completely. If you feel anything going out of place, or if you are unhappy with your parents' reactions and overall behavior, talk about it. Let them know that you don't like the way they swear in front of your kids, or the way they spend money without thinking about saving it. Whether or not it makes a difference, talking about your problems will help a lot in reducing your mental burden.

5. Correct them in love

It is essential to keep in mind that immature people have very fragile egos. When they do a wrong, they should be corrected but not, in the same manner, you would correct a mature person. Instead, get creative by ensuring that you do not blame them for the wrong or attack their own premise. Make your correction in the form of a suggestion such as "Don't you think it will be better if …'

6. Don't expect them to be different

It is always jarring to see an adult behave like a child, but you will keep getting disappointed if you refuse to accept that they are not going to change. Yes, they are old in years, but remember that they are probably stuck somewhere in middle school.

Stop expecting them to do better and instead make arrangements to compensate for any shortfall brought on by their behavior and move on.

7. Prevent them from throwing a tantrum

It is essential to learn how to preempt an immature person if you want to have a less fractious relationship with them. Make them realize that there is no reason for them to get their backs up at all. Say you asked a colleague on his way to the vending machine to get you a Kit Kat, and she starts complaining. Let her realize that she was already going to the vending machine anyway and that getting yours will only take an extra 20 seconds. By letting them understand how silly their reaction is, they tend to move on.

8. Give them space

It is quite tempting to keep correcting or managing an immature person all the time. A better way to deal with them, however, maybe to give them space and allow them to be. When there is no one to argue with or scream at, an immature person will more quickly realize their bad behavior and make necessary adjustments.

9.Take control

You will hardly ever please an immature person anyway, so you may as well stop worrying about hurting their overly delicate sensibilities and just take charge. Do not acknowledge their behavior or complaints. Just go ahead and do your thing. Your refusal to give them the attention they want may just make them realize that life is not all about them anyway and shut them up.

Notes:

Emotionally Immature Parents

Emotionally Immature Parents

Chapter 10: Reclaiming your freedom to be Yourself

Most of the time, we are the master of an ill-fitting role because we have been in it for so long. The details in this chapter explain how people feel when they wake up from what they have been doing wrong. The awakening stage is characterized by the presence of both physical and psychological symptoms such as depression, anxiety, sleeplessness, fear, and severe tension. When these symptoms set in, then we should be sure that we have been getting it wrong for a long time.

True Self

According to the studies carried out by psychologists among different populations in the world, it is believed that the reality of true self is that it is similar across culture. Its concept is that it is viewed as being moral and ethical. The true self is considered to be as old as the "self" itself and can be attributed to the time a person was born. Sometimes, our true self can also be referred to as the inner self, real self, or core self. In most cases, what we find ourselves doing is contrary to what our true self craves for and yet we keep doing it. Each person has a unique personality, and the interesting aspect of the true self is that it cannot be manipulated by the pressure of the environment, families, or even the way we act.

Sometimes, all we care about is how people perceive us, which leads to not knowing the exact person we are, and it gets to a stage that all we want to do is please people. You know your true self when you are conscious and aware of who you really are. The true self isn't the other-self you wish to be, rather, it is the exact person you are. The connection we have with our true self makes us see things as they are and feel more relaxed that we are on the right path. When we pay more attention to ourselves, we tend to be luckier as more opportunities come to us, and also people will want to be associated with people that are real.

The Demand of True Self

Like every attribute that we have, your true self doesn't want to be hidden; instead, it wants to be expressed. The main thing it demands is for you to eliminate negative thinking patterns and replace them with a positive and supportive mindset. Your true self wouldn't be satisfied with your current situation, but it will always encourage you to be better and fulfilled more genuinely. Most times, it is not interested in whatever the ideas that crept into your head while you were younger. The real demands of your true self are for the self-actualization of dreams through sincerity and honesty. This act makes your true self feel happier, successful, and fulfilled.

A child is usually influenced to be their authentic self when the adults around them encourage them to do so. They become in charge of their thoughts and tend to expose more of who they are. But when they are made to know life is all about bringing out your false self instead of your true self, pretense sets in, and all that matters to them is how they can please their parents and others in other to be loved. They deny their needs and desire while they turn off their true self and tread the path others lead them to and, in the process, play a role that isn't theirs.

There are a few things you can engage in to activate your true self.

Exercise: Waking Up Your True Self

This is one of the greatest adventures you can undergo in your lifetime. When you ignore your deepest needs, your true self ignites your emotional being to remind you that you have to take care of yourself. When you are aware of these emotional symptoms you get when you are drifting from your true self, you bounce back to who you used to be, then you see things as they really are.

The aim of this exercise is for you to awaken and be conscious of your true self. Wakening to your true self might be a wild thing to explore, but it is better for you in the long run. The materials required are a piece of paper and a pen. Fold the paper into two halves so that you can only use a side at a time. Write a heading that says: "My Role Self" and "My True Self," respectively, on each side of the paper.

Start with the heading "My true self." In this case, you have to be truthful and honest with yourself while you reminisce on your childhood days. Children are mostly influenced by the people and the environment they grew up in and are identified by the defenses of their parents, which affects the expression of the real personality of the individual. This stage requires being brave and willing to remember the things you did in the past, those things you cherished, and the things you were comfortable doing. Remembering these things takes you through the road of having a deep understanding of who you are and what you really stand for. Other things to put into consideration in the past include the things you enjoyed doing, the things you were good at, the type of people you loved to associate with, the reason you moved with them, what made you grow fond of them and the kind of sport you enjoyed playing (indoor or outdoor). These analyses should be done without the consideration of money as it may be a confounder, which can stand against honesty. When you have written the necessary things, move on to the next page.

Write the heading "My Role Self" on the next page. This phase acts like a self-assessment which is required to provide information on your personality and who you have grown to become in the past years and is a justification for the new way you act, what is the attitude you have put up in other to be loved and appreciated. Do the things you do make you happy or do you do them primarily to please people? Do you feel comfortable with the people you have around you? What are the things you do, and do they interest you or bore you? Do you care more about what people say about you than what you feel about yourself?

At the end of the assessment, put the piece of paper aside for some days, after which you open it up and straighten the paper. Then compare both sides and assess yourself. Are you fulfilled, and do you do what your true self desires by checking your role self, or do you do what is contrary to your true self?

Breaking Down To Awaken

When people live outside their true self, and the influence of their role self reduces, they begin to experience a breakdown. Psychological growth can be affected by how we have been expressing ourselves and it can be either frustrating or fulfilling depending on the path you choose. Sometimes we go through a breakdown, and everything that comes to our mind during this period is self-pity. It is not a bad idea to feel sorry for oneself, but in most cases, that should not be the first resort. The first thing you should entertain in such a situation is to know the cause of the breakdown. When we think forth, we resolve to the fact that we are responsible for the breakdown when in the real sense, it is caused by the inability to keep up with the emotional lies which brought us down rather than the truth that could have held us up. There are varieties of things that can break us down, but for the context of this book, we will consider emotional unconsciousness and distress.

When you begin to feel emotionally unstable with the acts you have put up, and it seems you have broken down, then you should know that your true self wants to find a way to creep out. Your true self starts by waking you up and letting you know that the emotional immaturity of your parents will not give you the best life you desire. Instead, you have to free yourself and find out your true self-ignoring who you have been made to believe you are.

According to Jean Piaget (1963), for people to hold on to new things, their initial belief of the matter must be allowed to break up and rework itself for the knowledge. The process of breaking down and waking up helps you discover yourself. Kazimierz Dabrowski (1972) believed that emotional distress should be viewed as a sign of growth and not illness, except in a few cases.

Awakening From Playing Role Self

For how long can people play the role-self game, maybe into adulthood but never for too long. There comes a time where you wouldn't feel the need to impress people or to go out of your way to be accepted. When you feel like this, then you have gotten a wakeup call which comes alongside emotional symptoms. The change can be quite obvious and sometimes unaccepted by your immature parents.

Release Yourself from a Self-Defeating Role

Grab a note pad and write a short and precise description of a person in your life who makes you feel anxious or affect your self-esteem. Then, write down how you feel and act when you are with that person, do you think you are yourself with the person? or do you pretend to get along well with him/her? Do you wish this person would act differently towards you, and for how long have you been expecting a change? Are you willing to let this person know your true self and the way you want them to treat you?

Waking Up To What You Really Feel

Sometimes we find ourselves accepting what we wouldn't give room for on a normal day. We feel guilty for the things that are unacceptable to our true self. We have believed that the only way to impress people is to accept every stone they throw at us. However, if we suppress our feelings for a long time, we eventually turn to take a look at what is wrong.

Exploring Whether You Have Hidden Feelings

There are times you feel anxious and down for no particular reason within your reach. The truth is that there is a reason behind whatever you think. Check yourself and consider if you are holding on to anything or anyone that's making you have such feelings. Another thing that can be helpful is for you to remember when you had such a feeling and relate it back to the things/persons that prompted such feelings.

If a person is responsible for the feelings, write down your emotions straightforwardly and transparently. You can do this privately to avoid distractions and other people's influence on your decision. Politely, speak to yourself about what you don't like concerning the person. Is it the way the person addresses you or the way you feel the person treats you? When you voice those things out, you feel better and release the tension that has built up.

You don't need to confront the person concerning his/her act. The goal is for you to feel better and not embark on a hatred journey. Confrontation can come later when you feel better and have a free mind concerning the person.

Waking Up Through Relationship Breakdown

Experience in the world of psychotherapy has made me realize that relationship problems are an essential wake-up tool. Being that we display painful patterns that we were taught during childhood into our adult relationships. When we do not get our emotional needs met, they become unresolved issues. In intimate adult relationships, sometimes we project our parent's issues onto our partners, and unconsciously, we become angry with them.

Waking Up from Idealizing Others

Most cultures make us believe parents know better, or even in the real sense, they are wiser. This unproven theory was only backed up with age. Also, when children become adults, the environment does not make them acknowledge their mistakes and weaknesses. Sometimes, it is evident that they are wrong, but the idea we have grown to believe is that their mistakes should be endured not pointed out because all of their acts can be justified. Unfortunately, it is because we don't want them to feel vulnerable, but the truth still stands that they cannot always be correct.

Waking Up to Your Strengths

When you think of working on your weaknesses, you should also appreciate your strength. However, children brought up by immature parents have a contrary experience of such. Their positive qualities are usually not dwelt upon or appreciated because such parents cannot see the strength of their children. This has resulted in making the children embarrassed of every quality they possess. They are used to encouraging the good qualities of others and feel it is wrong for their own strength to be pointed out.

The fact that your parents do not see your strength doesn't mean you shouldn't see it either.

Identify your good qualities and embrace them. Know what you stand for and the positive virtues you possess. However, to stand in the phase for a long time, you have to be honest and modest in everything.

Waking Up to Forget Childhood Issues

Consciously or the other way round, we have had childhood emotional injuries. Realizing and working through these psychological injuries is a way of waking up and healing. According to a study by Cassidy et al., it is found out that parents who raise kids that are securely attached are always willing to talk about their own childhood. Although some of them do not have pleasant childhood experiences, however, they made their children feel secure. These parents know what it feels like to have emotional injuries and will do their best to ensure their children do not face the same dilemma.

10.1 Living Your Own Life Free From An Emotionally Immature Parent

Family Patterns That Could Be a Source of Hindrance to Your Growth

Before we explore ways of living a life free of roles and responsibilities, it's essential to look into the patterns that could be holding you back from living your life for yourself. Some of them include:

Disapproval of Individuality

If an emotionally unstable or immature parent raised you, the chances are that you spent your young life walking on eggshells. Rather than being allowed to be yourself, express your opinion, act your natural self, you are forced to mirror their actions, thoughts, opinions, and lifestyle even if they go against what you believe in or the way you would want to speak or act. An emotionally immature parent due to their own insecurities and fears prefer the predictable kind of life that you have been taught.

These parents are scared and threatened by their children's individuality; they are afraid when their children express themselves or act in their own best interest because it breaks the predictable pattern they are used to. Therefore, the children, in turn, rather than making their parents anxious because of their actions and words, would rather suppress their individuality and pretend to be who they are not, just to give their parents a sense of security.

In such cases, children are often ashamed to express the following emotions:

- Spontaneity

- Enthusiasm

- Grief/sadness/sorrow

- Expressing their innermost thoughts

- Affection

On the other hand, they are thought something else entirely, and these include:

- Absolute obedience to authority

- A physical illness that allows the parents to exhibit their authority

- Self-doubt

- Liking what the parents like and vice versa

- Shame over being imperfect

- Ability to listen to their parent's complaints and distress

- Stereotyped gender roles and responsibilities

If you have an emotionally immature parent and you were an internalizing child, then you would have been taught a lot of self-defeating things that ought to help you get along in life. Some of these things include:

- First consider what others want from you

- Never speak up for yourself

- Don't ever ask others for help

- Be satisfied and don't ask for more

Internalizing children have been taught by their emotionally immature parents that 'goodness' is synonymous with being self-effacing and that their parents' demands must be met first before anyone else. They see their desires and feelings as unimportant or shameful. However, once they come to see it for what it is (a distorted mindset), then it becomes easier to set things right.

Sticking To an Internalized Parental Voice

You may wonder how parents can train their children to go against their gut instincts or feelings, but this is not only possible, but it is natural. Sometimes, when we find ourselves wanting to do something or take a particular action, there is that inner voice echoing in your mind. Now while you may think this is your inner voice speaking to you, it is the voice of your early caregivers talking through a process called parent-voice internalization. This voice may make unkind comments concerning your self-worth, intelligence, and character.

The fact is that everyone internalizes their parent's voice, while some are lucky to have been brought by very supportive and friendly parents and hence have positive parent-voice internalization, others are not so fortunate and so have pessimistic parent-voice internalization. However, there is a need to break out of this pessimistic parent-voice internalization as only then can you truly know your self-worth and not judge yourself based on their critical evaluation. The aim is to identify the voice as a foreign language and not part of your own thinking. This is done by using the maturity awareness approach already discussed in chapter eight to relate with the negative voices just the same way you will use the same method with your parents.

You are Free to Be Human and Imperfect

It is most likely that an internalized parental voice gets its origin from the left hemisphere, a region where language and logic are dominated. When this left brain is allowed to do its job, it chooses efficiency and perfectionism before feelings, judgment, and compassion (McGilchrist 2009). Without the right side of the brain, which is the personal and intuitive part, your left brain is like a machine that uses the equation of right and wrong to access you. It will inform you when you are good, bad, broken, or perfect, and this is done according to your achievement. This kind of assessment is an aspect of mental rigidity that is associated with emotional immaturity.

You are Free to Suspend Contract

I am confident you will like to have the freedom to be yourself while also protecting yourself when it comes to your relationship with your parents. Yet, there are times you will need to suspend contact even if it's for a while to save your emotional health. This is likely to stir up self-doubt and guilt, but when you consider what you stand to gain by doing this, and then there will be no room for guilt. Some parents are hurtful and disrespectful of their children's boundaries, and even after repeated explanations as to why it's not acceptable, they still don't get it. Perhaps because they relish being difficult or possibly because it's the only way they know, either way, in such a situation, it's necessary to keep your distance for a while.

You Are Free To Set Your Limits and To Choose How Much You Can Give

While suspending contact is effective, some people are also able to set limits and stick to it such that their parents do not have the avenue to do them more harm. This can be done by limiting the frequency of your contact with them. When you set a limit on your contact with your parents, you are then able to dedicate more time to your self-care. You may feel guilty and selfish at first. However, this time gives you the opportunity you may have for choosing yourself and your mental health over your emotionally immature parents.

You Are Free Not To Be Excessively Compassionate

One of the problems of being an internalized person is that such people can feel excessively compassionate for other people's problems; they tend to end up feeling worse than the person perceived to have the problem. What is needed is a healthy empathic feeling; this helps you be compassionate and yet not lose focus of your own limit.

You Are Free To Take Action on Your Own Behalf

If you grew up with emotionally immature parents, there's the tendency of you feeling helpless as though no one can help you and that you don't deserve to be helped unless someone offers that help at their own discretion.

It should be noted that such upbringing can be very traumatic and can transcend to your adult life such that you have feelings of not being able to do anything or not deserving of help. You may feel like a victim with no control and at the mercy of others who may not want to give what you crave for.

However, you can regain your freedom from this kind of feeling no matter how ingrained in you it may seem. You can take action on your own behalf as this is the antidote to the feeling of helplessness. Indeed, emotionally immature parents do not give you a good picture of what life and relationships have to offer, but I hope that you are starting to realize that your possibilities are endless and that you owe yourself a duty to ask what you want.

You Are Free To Express Yourself

When you express yourself with emotionally immature parents, it's a form of self-affirmation and an assertion that you exist as an individual with your own feeling and thoughts. It's essential to let go of the idea that if your parents loved you, they would understand you, you may never have that kind of relationship with them, and that's ok. What you need to focus on is making sure that each conversation with them is satisfying for you.

You are free to speak politely, to express yourself without having to make excuses. When you show yourself to them in this form, then you are being your true self even if they do not understand.

You Are Free To Approach Old Relationships in a New Way

You have the freedom to converse with your parents in a new way and shake up their old patterns. They may react in a more emotionally genuine way, or they could become worse, but then they may open up more when you stop wanting them to change. When they see how strong you have become without the need for their approval, they may begin to relax. If you stop expecting them to change, then the chances are that they will be able to accept more openness.

This will only happen when you stop expecting them to change or act in a certain way, and even at that, these changes may not occur at all, no matter what you do. However, you must stay true to yourself, stay emotionally detached, and expect nothing from them. When you expect nothing from them, you give them the freedom to be their true selves while you, on the other hand, also maintain your real personality.

Notes:

Emotionally Immature Parents

Emotionally Immature Parents

Chapter 11: Healing (Specialist and Self-Help)

Having physically but emotionally unavailable parents is one of the worst experiences a child may deal with. Children with these kinds of parents may be affected in numerous ways. Those who have it worse tend to depend on substances as a means of getting rid of the pain.

For your life to become how you want it to be, you will have to go through the process of recovery. Everyone may have suffered differently, but the healing process typically involves the same things, and we will be looking into all of these. Below is a list of things you can do to get your life back on track completely.

Observe more, react less

Instead of trying to make your parents understand where they went wrong, try convincing yourself why it is time you should let it go. Use your power of thinking and reasoning to rationalize the negative thoughts and stop yourself from being an emotional victim anymore. Repeat these three things to yourself every day:

- I have 'myself'

- I don't need approval from others for what I do

- I know I am doing my best

Let it pass

Stop acting like parents to your parents. If you feel something is not right, express without fear and then let it go. Your parents might likely give you unexpected and extreme reactions, just stay calm and establish your point with determination.

Focus on the outcome

It may be impractical to expect empathy and understanding from immature parents, considering their level of perception and emotional intelligence. What you can do instead is decide on how do you want to see your relationship with your parents. For instance, if you don't want your parents to know that they made you feel bad at some point, do not talk about it and maintain a safe distance. Stay connected with them, but on some level, figure out your escape from falling into the emotional hazards again.

Accept and Move On

The physical age of immature parents cannot be equated with their maturity level. Accept this and remember it whenever you are having a conversation with them. You may have to talk to them like you would to your teenager at home. Instead of getting side-tracked by their reactions and complaints, stick to your point and make things work the way you want them to.

Detach Yourself from Your Emotionally Immature Parents

Your parents raised you, so it is normal for them to have become a significant part of your life. Regardless of if you know it or not, they are a very crucial part of you. This is mostly because of the way they condition you and unconsciously urge you to mirror their behavior. Even if you did not mean to, you probably wouldn't have been able to help but behave like those who raised you.

You need to begin your healing here. You need to let go of all you have learned from your parents, as this will help you free up your mind for the healing process. Remember that this will be one of the most challenging things you can do. Unlearning all you have learned so far is not an easy task, but it is possible. This is what makes it one of the most important things to do to accomplish your healing.

If you are still finding it difficult to let go of these parents, remember the kind of damage and toxicity they bring to you. You need to give priority to your health and well-being. If you are serious about living a healthy life, then you must detach from them completely.

Let Go of the Self-blame

You may believe that your parents are the way they are because of something you did. No, that is just how they are made, and it is not your fault in any way. Nothing is wrong with you, and you have to realize this fact. They were not able to create a genuine emotional connection with you because they lacked the capacity and not because you were worthless. You deserved love and attention as a kid, and your parents were unable to provide you with it. They were adults, and you had no say in the kind of behavior they exhibited. Another form of self-blame you may have gotten used to is blaming yourself for things that don't go your way even when it is not your fault. This is because your parents may have accused you and made you feel the same over the years. You need to be kind to yourself and avoid this form of self-blame as it only makes matters worse for you.

There are many ways you can show kindness to yourself. Some of these are:

- Talk to yourself the way you would a close friend. If you had a friend in a similar situation as you, what would you say to them?

How would you treat them? Now treat yourself in the same manner. Be a best friend to yourself.

- Acknowledge all of the things you feel. However, don't hold on to them or dwell on them.

- Understand that you are not the only one dealing with pain. Everyone suffers pain at some point. But the difference is how you deal with this pain.

- Anytime you want to blame or criticize yourself, take note of the voice you hear. Is it coming from you, or are your emotionally immature parents speaking through you? If the voice isn't yours, you have to detach yourself from it and think about how you feel about the matter. Once you have established this fact with yourself, you can now move on to seeing your parents as who they are.

Face the Reality of Your Parents

We already discussed how to let go of your childish fantasies in the earlier chapters regarding how things will get better. You may still be holding on to the ideology that your parents will become the type of parents you want them to be.

Doing this will only leave you feeling disappointed and sad because this is something that will never come true. Your emotionally immature parents can't change and probably never will. The instant you can accept that your parents can only offer you all that is within their capacity, you allow yourself to heal. And if you choose to have them in your life still, you can have a relationship with them within their limitations, and this will make sure you don't face any disappointments. The power to determine the type of relationship you want with your parents is solely dependent on you. Weigh your options accurately and decide whether you want these toxic parents in your life or not.

Give Yourself the Chance to Grieve

You know the pain and frustration that comes from having emotionally immature parents. This is the moment to let yourself grieve so you can get better. To do this, pick an activity that correctly gives you the chance to let it all out. There is no single strategy for grieving, so you are free to choose one that works for you. Things that require you to use your hands and creativity are great options to try out. These could range from sculpting, writing, painting, and so on. Understandably, you crave the attention of your parents. This is the desire of every child, so it does not make you abnormal. Although you might feel some anger and bitterness towards your emotionally immature parents for being unable to give you the kind of connection you deserved, you need to acknowledge your feelings and let it go. Many emotionally immature parents make their children feel bad for trying to express their feelings. This would most likely have been the case with you, and over time, it probably has become a part of you. A great way of acknowledging your feelings is to draw out all those things you felt and neglected over the years. If you search deeply, you will realize these feelings never really left. All you have to do is let yourself feel them. Once you do, acknowledge them and give yourself the chance to grieve how you want to. This will help you on your path to recovery. The next thing you need to do once you have acknowledged these feelings is to get to know yourself.

Knowing Yourself

A repercussion of the constant shaming, down-talking, and criticism your emotionally immature parents dish out to you is often that you forget who you are. As we covered in an earlier chapter, many children may adopt a role-self that will allow them to fit into the family dynamics of the emotionally immature parents. If you fall into this category, you will probably have let go of who you are over time. We took a look at how to find your true self once before in chapter 3, so feel free to refer to it for more guidance. As you begin to understand your feelings once more, do not hold any resentment, instead determine all of your needs, grieve, and move on. The last part of knowing yourself is to pay attention to those things you feel. Doing this will help you understand everything you think. It will also help you determine your innate needs and wants. To do this, pay attention to your body. Our bodies are built to naturally let us know those things we desire even if we don't know it. Determine the emotion you are feeling and the effect it has on your body. Learn to determine your feelings and also take time to reflect on them. All of these will help you better understand the type of person you are, and those things you genuinely desire.

If you are stuck trying to determine your true self and your needs, try providing answers to the following questions:

Determining Your Needs

- Do you want attention?

- Do you want to be listened to?

- Do you want someone to love you and make you feel safe?

- Do you want to create a genuine emotional connection with others?

- Do you have self-development needs?

- What are your spiritual needs?

Once you have figured out the answers to these questions, you will be able to determine your precise needs. These needs won't be those planted by your emotionally immature parents but your needs alone.

Find a Way to Forgive

It is understandable for you to be bitter and resent your emotionally immature parents. This feeling is most likely going to become more evident once you become one with your emotions. However, if you are serious about recovering completely, forgiveness is not optional. You are not doing this for the benefit of your parents, but for your benefit. Learning to forgive and to let go will help you move forward.

If you continue to let yourself feel resentment and anger, you are never going to let go of your experience. However, forgiving your emotionally immature parent does not imply that you are validating the behavior of your parents; it merely means you have moved on. Forgive your parents, and you will open up the path of healing for yourself.

Develop Skills to Help You Calm Yourself

When emotionally immature parents raise you, you don't get the soothing you need as a child. This is because of their inability to create real emotional connections. However, just because your parents failed to teach you how to express your emotions and calm yourself properly, it does not mean you can't correct it yourself.

Depending on the kind of person you are, there are many ways you can calm yourself. The following are some of the main options you can leverage:

- Take a walk through nature and focus on living in the now. Take in all you can and experience everything to the fullest.

- Engage in mindful breathing. To do this, inhale as deep as you can, then exhale as long as possible. Put in efforts into exhaling and count to 5 or 10 while you exhale.

- Listen to calming music. Choose slow-paced music as opposed to fast ones as they are more likely to calm and soothe you.

- Watch funny videos or check out images that will make you laugh. When you laugh, it releases endorphins in your body. This is a natural chemical that makes you feel good. By releasing these chemicals, you can feel better, and in some instances, it can even alleviate pain.

- Surround yourself with things that help you relax. These could include scents and objects that calm you.

Recreate Your Boundaries

With emotionally immature parents, boundaries are not respected in the lives of their kids. If these kinds of parents raised you, you might have adopted this behavior in your adult life. You may be exhausted and angry at all times due to your inability to set up boundaries.

However, if your parents are still a part of your life, you need to learn to set your boundaries with them. This will give you the reassurance that your life is yours alone. You alone make the choices, and if your parents have always controlled your life, then this is an excellent way to get your freedom.

The following are some of the other ways to set your boundaries:

- Begin to say "No" during those instances you said "Yes" and started having regrets later.

- Before you do anything for anyone, ask yourself: "Is this truly okay with me?"

- Don't forget that you are as crucial as every other person around you, and this means you are allowed to set boundaries. Even more important is the fact that your boundaries have to be respected by others.

Hang Around People Who Love You

Spending time around people who have a genuine interest in mind can help accelerate your healing. Some of these could include your friends, family members, or even co-workers.

Check out the friends you have presently and determine those who make you feel good. Let go of the people around you who don't make you feel happy. Also, let go of people who use you to meet their own needs. Whether you want to admit it or not, there will be people who you call friends that only stay friends with you for their benefit. You need to let go of them.

Instead, spend time around people who support you and want the best for you too.

Get Professional Help

Finally, if you don't seem to be making any headway on your own, getting help from a professional is the way to go. Going to therapy with a therapist who understands the effect of dealing with an emotionally immature parent can help you heal faster.

A therapist can see things from a professional perspective. He or she is trained to notice things that you may have missed and even determine the best route to help you get your healing.

However, you need to note that therapy only works if you are open and can completely trust your therapist. You need to be ready to open up and let the professionals in, and with time, you can deal with everything you have held inside.

Emotionally Immature Parents

Notes:

Chapter 12: How to recognize an Emotionally Mature Relationship

Dealing with immature people brings to the fore how relevant emotional intelligence is in dealing with people. It is a life skill that will not only help you keep friends, but also aid in your career advancement and attaining goals.

Here are five ways you can consciously work on getting emotional intelligence.

Control your own negative emotions: A common quote is that "you can't control all that happens to you in life, but you can control how you react to it." This is the foundation of taking charge of negative emotions. Maybe someone jumped you in a queue, instead of getting riled up and allowing that to ruin your morning, consider that they are probably rushing off to get to a sick child. Be objective at all times and consider issues from different perspectives before reacting. Whenever the pressure of work (and your colleagues) is getting at you, take a few minutes to practice mindfulness. It will help you be in charge of your reaction to situations.

Choose your words carefully: The words you choose in communication will become a crucial factor in the kind of result you will get. Learn to use positive words in getting your point across to people around you. If your boss delegated a task to you without prior notice, do not say 'I can't do it' but rather 'I'm going to try my best'. When a misunderstanding arises, go back to the events that occurred before it devolved into an argument and think of better words you could have used to defuse the situation.

Show empathy: Empathy is one of the essential forms of effective communication known to the modern man. From body language, eye movement, hand gestures, and the like, you get to understand what people are not telling you and avoid sticky situations. Remember that everyone is fighting battles even though you may not know about it and show empathy to everyone around you.

Recognize the things that stress you: It is quite easy to fly off the handle when you are stressed and tired than when relaxed. To this end, look for ways to reduce stressors to a minimum. If getting to work late messes up your schedule and turns you into a grouch, then start setting your alarm 30 minutes early. Don't skip lunch in favor of getting more work done when you know that hunger gives you a migraine. As you manage stress more effectively, you will be happier and have better relationships with those around you.

Dealing with Immaturity in A Relationship

You may have been swept off your feet by a suave, confident, and attractive person and started a relationship only to realize that they are immature. The good clothes, carriage, and projected confidence are just facades for a child in the body of an adult. Dealing with such a person requires tact and honesty with yourself. Here are ways you can do that:

- Accept that you cannot change them: Most often, when we encounter people with bad behavior, we assume that our own innate goodness will influence them into becoming better people as they follow our example. This is not always true. An immature adult may never grow up, so don't delude yourself by believing that they are going to change someday.

•Be honest with yourself: Take time to ask yourself where you see the relationship going. Is there a possibility that this person will want to settle down? If they do, are you sure that you will be able to live with them? If your relationship is not just about having a good time, you may want to decide whether to continue with this person or end it.

•Start a conversation: It is effortless for immature people to get defensive. Despite this, it is essential to talk to them. Let them know the habits you are not cool with or which embarrass you. If you want them to help out more, let them know. Get your own feelings out there. It may give an immature partner a rethink of some of their actions. If your partner refuses to listen, you may need to bring in a counselor.

- **Be assertive:** The only way to deal with someone interested in getting their own way is to be assertive. Remain polite and understanding but pass your message across very clearly whenever you are communicating.

- **Do not go to their level:** Have you ever seen two toddlers fighting over a stick of candy? Not cute, right? Exactly. You may be tempted to behave in an immature manner, too; after all, two can play that game. Do not do this. Behaving, as an immature partner does will only bring more problems into your relationship. Act like an adult.

- **Stop making excuses for your partner:** It is human nature to want to present our partners as good people to others. This may make you start explaining his behavior away to others. Do not make excuses for your partner when they act or speak out of turn. Leave them to solve any problem they create by themselves. Trying to help an immature partner smoothen things over with others will make them not to learn from his mistakes.

•Be patient: Be patient when dealing with an immature partner. The truth is that you are going to get so exasperated you may get tempted to pull your hair out. Try to support him as much as you can, be there for him, especially when such partners show interest in changing for better. Take it one day at a time.

•Get the help you need: You may try all you can to improve your relationship without positive results. In this case, it is better to seek the assistance of a certified therapist or counselor to help you improve your relationship and assist your partner work on their behavior.

Attributes of emotionally mature people

Emotionally Mature People are Reliable and Realistic

Realistic and reliable may sound humdrum, but nothing beats someone with this foundation. It's just like a house; the color doesn't matter; what matters is the structure of the building, for without a firm foundation, the house falls like a pack of cards. The same applies to a healthy relationship; a good relationship should feel like a well-designed house, easy to enter and exit without much thought to the planning and architecture put into it.

Emotionally Mature People Work with Reality Rather Than Fight Reality

These sets of people are continually working to change the things they don't like but are always aware of the reality in their own terms. When problems arise, they try and fix rather than overreacting or obsessing on how things should be, and if things aren't working out a planned, they just make the best out of the situation.

They Think and Feel Simultaneously

An emotionally mature person can think even when upset, and that's someone you can reason with. These people can't reason with other people and see a different perspective, also when things aren't going as planned. They are focused and don't lose track of emotional factors when they are addressing an issue.

They Are Consistent, Hence Reliable

These people will not spring inconsistent surprises on you as they have an integrated sense of self; they are predictable to an extent and can be counted upon to be the same in different situations. They can be trusted as their consistency makes them so trustworthy.

They Are Not Overly Sensitive

Emotionally mature people are not so touchy and don't take things too personally; they can laugh and take a joke even if they are the subject of such jokes. They are realistic enough to know they are not perfect; hence they see themselves as infallible even while doing the best they can.

People who take things too personally are either people with low self-esteem or a narcissist; these traits are not healthy as they always lead people to seek validation from others. This is not all; they also tend to think they are being evaluated at every given point and see criticisms where they are not, and they are always on the defensive.

They Are Respectful and Reciprocate

With emotionally mature people, everyone is worthy of respect and is treated fairly; they have a corporative orientation, which is evident from all the traits they possess and in how they treat others. They give you a feeling that they look out for you rather than being focused on their own self.

They Respect Boundaries

Emotionally mature people are very courteous, respectful, and honor boundaries. They are in search of connection and not an invasion. These people do not assume that since you love them, then you love what they love too. Instead, they take your feelings and desires into consideration; they are in tune with how others feel. Though this may seem like a lot, to them, it's as natural as breathing in air.

One of the attributes of a healthy relationship is one in which you are not told what to do or how to feel. If you grew up with emotionally immature parents, then you are probably used to unsolicited advice and analysis from others. This is usually the case that in themselves have problems and are looking for ways to use others to make themselves feel good. Rather than stick with these kinds of people, it's best to migrate to those who respect you for who you are.

Emotionally Mature People Give Back

Rather than take advantage of you, emotionally mature people are generous and always want to help out, they are generous with their time while at the same time asking for help when they need it. They are still willing to give more than they get back, but in all they do, they try to create a balance between things.

With emotionally immature parents, they have trained you to either give too much or too little; they are always demanding, and this will have an effect on you in the long run. If you grew up an internalizer, you would believe that to gain the world's approval; you have to keep giving and giving despite being drained or getting nothing in return.

Compromise

These people try to be fair, objective, and flexible. One of the traits to look out in people with whether or not they are emotionally mature is how they respond to change in plans. You should watch out if these people can differentiate between a rejection and a sudden change of plans. Are they able to express their disappointment without trying to blame you? If a situation comes up and you can't stick to plan will they understand, will you be given the benefit of the doubt? Will they be empathic and compromising?

Emotionally mature people are aware that disappointments and changes are a normal phenomenon in life, rather than dwell on their disappointments they look for alternatives and solutions; they are open to ideas and won't blame you for what you have no control over.

Rather than have you bring all, they meet you halfway. In contrast, the reverse is the case for emotionally immature people who always pressure others into concessions that they alone stand to benefit from.

Other Attributes of Emotionally Mature People

The list of positive attributes of emotionally mature people are endless, some other attributes which they possess include:

- They have an even temper

- They don't mind being influenced
- They don't lie
- They don't hesitate to apologize and make amends
- They are responsive
- You are safe in their empathy
- They see and understand you
- They comfort and like to be comforted too
- They are optimists; laughing freely and being playful
- They are fun to be with

Moving from Immaturity to Emotional Maturity

"Where there is a will, there is a way" is a popular saying that points out how anything is possible to a person that is determined. Even an immature person can, with time, consciously develop emotional intelligence. It is possible to grow and become better if they make efforts to improve with the situations and people they encounter daily.

Be present

To become emotionally mature, be present in your own life. Stays attuned to your feelings and notice the areas in your life where you have been behaving childishly. Notice the areas people always complain about and choose to make a positive change.

Note the triggers

While you remain present to everything around you, take note of the things that bring about immature reactions from you. Are there family members that get your goat all the time? Is there a specific language that raises your hackles? Knowing your triggers and why that thing irritates, you can help you in responding differently.

Accept reality

Life is not fair. Accept this and take action to work on the things that are within your control. When you accept that terrible thing happens, that disappointments and trials are all a part of life and living, you will not look for people to blame when things don't go your way. You will not whine or throw tantrums when an opportunity falls through. Instead, you will take a step back and review everything that happened intending to make corrections that will improve your chances the next time you try.

Take responsibility

As an adult, you are always responsible for all of your actions and reactions. When you decide to think things through and always respond in the way that aligns with the greater good of all, you are taking back your willpower and owning it.

Stop that instinctive inclination to respond to hurts, disappointments, and slurs based on the way you feel. Instead, ask yourself, 'What will my reaction/response say about me?' why is the other person attacking me? What is the other person's story?

Decide whom you want to be

Many people go through life without ever being their authentic selves. Ask searching questions of yourself and decide on the answers that will enable you to face yourself in the mirror without flinching. What do you want to be remembered for? What one word do you want others to use in describing you? Once you decide on all these things, it becomes easier to determine how to behave in every situation.

Dealing with an immature person takes a lot of maturities. Even when you recognize the signs and try to correct them, they may not be receptive to it. Be patient and fix them only in love, be assertive when you have to and never go down to their level. Know that, ultimately, an immature person can take practical steps to improve and become better if they choose to.

Emotionally Immature Parents

Notes:

CONCLUSION

Congratulations! You have made it to the end of the book. This only goes to show how serious you are about getting your life back together. The pain of having a parent who is unable to create any real emotional connection is incomparable. It can also affect your life in many more ways than one.

Still, this does not mean that it is something that can't be corrected. With the information I have provided in this book, you can quickly fix the damage and begin to live the life you deserve.

Never forget that you are not responsible for the situation you have found yourself in. You do not fault the issue, and you are not unworthy. Emotionally immature parents cannot give you all you want as a child, and this is just how they are built. Instead of looking for ways to change them into your perfect definition of parents, invest that time into your healing.

Filling up the emotional void left behind by your parents can take a while. This makes it essential for you to start as soon as you can. The more time you take, the more damage it causes to your life and that of your kids if you have any. Take all the necessary measures you can to free yourself from the effects of the emotional negligence of your parents.

This is not a process that happens overnight. It requires work, but I assure you that it will all be worth it in the end when you retake control of your life.

You are strong, you are a survivor, and you can beat this. See you at the top of this minor setback, living the type of life you desire.

From being a child to having a child, the parent-child relationship is equally impactful through all the stages of life. Although dealing with parental immaturity may be difficult when we are young, but acknowledging the fact and keeping our expectations grounded can bring significant improvement in the bond we share with them. We, as children, must not stop empathizing with our parents just because they don't. Instead, we can start trying to:

- Communicate more often - Never letting our parents feel unloved and unwanted.

- Spend more time - Planning for trips and day outs where we can work on bridging the gap that has been there for years.

- Recollect old memories together - Going through old albums and talking about those childhood days we spent with them, resurrecting only the old happy times.

Nurturing the relationship we have with parents is an art of living - it helps us in becoming a better person by letting go of what hurts us and making way for a happier and positive life. We must remember that no matter how our parents are, they always did the best they could. They might have been too young to feel our pain, or too stressed to notice our hurdles, but at the end of the day, they mean the world to us - and we, to them.

I hope you had useful information by reading Emotionally Immature Parents. Please let me know your sincere thoughts by leaving a short review on Amazon. Thank you.

Emotionally Immature Parents

www.ingramcontent.com/pod-product-compliance
Lightning Source LLC
Chambersburg PA
CBHW071354210526
45465CB00001B/84